ESSENTIALS OF COIN COLLECTING FOR BEGINNERS

TIMELESS GUIDE TO FIND VALUABLE COINS, UNDERSTAND GRADING, AVOID COUNTERFEITS, AND TURN PASSION INTO PROFITS

DAVID GREEN

COPYRIGHT

CONTENTS

INTRODUCTION

Hello and welcome! If you've ever marveled at a beautifully minted coin and wondered about the stories it could tell or the value it might hold, you're in the right place. I'm thrilled to share the captivating world of coin collecting with you, a journey that extends far beyond mere hobby to embrace both history and investment.

My own adventure with coins began on a lazy Sunday afternoon at a small flea market. Rummaging through a box of old trinkets, my fingers brushed against a silver coin with an intricate design. As I held it up to the light, its details shimmered, and I felt an instant connection to its past owners and the history it represented. That moment of discovery was not just thrilling—it was transformative. It sparked a passion that has since grown into both a profound hobby and a fruitful investment avenue.

In "Essentials of Coin Collecting for Beginners," my goal is straightforward: to equip you, the beginner, with the knowledge and tools necessary to start your own coin-collecting journey with confidence. This book will guide you through the nuances of identifying valuable coins, understanding the critical aspects of grading, recognizing counterfeits, and, importantly, turning your growing passion into a potential source of income.

What sets this guide apart from others is its tailored approach for you—the middle-income, investment-oriented individual with a zest for history. It melds historical insights with practical, actionable advice, ensuring that you gain not just knowledge but also the skills to apply it effectively.

As we progress, you can expect a clear, step-by-step exploration of the coin-collecting world. From uncovering the most sought-after coins to navigating the vibrant community of collectors, each chapter is designed to build your understanding and enhance your collecting skills.

Perhaps most importantly, this book is an invitation—an invitation to view coin collecting not just as a pastime but as a gateway to a richer understanding of history and a viable investment opportunity. It's about more than coins; it's about discovering a passion that can enrich your life in myriad ways.

So, I invite you now to turn the page and begin this exciting journey. Dive into the first chapter with an open mind and an eagerness to explore, and let's uncover the treasures that await in the fascinating world of coin collecting.

Happy collecting!

CHAPTER ONE

THE BASICS OF COIN COLLECTING

Did you know that the first coins were minted in the 7th century BC in Lydia, now part of modern-day Turkey? These ancient artifacts were not only a means of trade but also a profound expression of art and a pivotal tool in the development of commerce. This fascinating blend of history, art, and economics is what draws many to coin collecting. Whether you find yourself captivated by the historical tales each coin tells or you see an opportunity for a prudent investment, understanding the basics of coin collecting is your first step toward becoming a proficient numismatist.

In this chapter, you'll explore how to choose your coin-collecting path, understand essential terms, set up your collecting space, and manage your budget. Each section is designed to build a strong foundation for your collecting endeavors, ensuring you approach this hobby with knowledge and enthusiasm.

CHOOSING YOUR COIN COLLECTING PATH

Coin collecting offers a unique duality—a fusion of historical appreciation and potential financial gain. Some collectors are drawn to coins for their rich historical value, collecting pieces that have witnessed the rise and fall of empires or served as silent observers to pivotal moments in history. Others view numismatics as a strategic investment, seeking coins whose value might appreciate over time.

Understanding why you are drawn to coin collecting is crucial. If history captivates you, you might find yourself drawn to ancient coins or those from specific historical periods. On the other hand, if investment is your primary motivation, you might focus on rare editions or bullion coins that are likely to increase in value due to their metal content or rarity.

Balancing Passion and Profit

The true art of coin collecting lies in balancing your passion for history with viable financial outcomes. For those who are history enthusiasts, it can be rewarding to delve into the stories behind a coin—like a copper penny from the Civil War era or a controversial commemorative coin. However, to turn coin collecting into a profitable venture, it's essential to stay informed about the market trends and understand what makes a coin valuable. This might mean choosing coins that, while historically significant, are also rare enough to demand higher prices in the market.

Setting realistic goals is essential, whether you're collecting coins for their historical value, potential investment returns, or a combination of both. Begin by defining what success looks like for you. Is it completing a collection of all minted versions of a historic coin? Or perhaps acquiring a set of coins that are projected to increase in value? Setting clear, achievable goals will help guide your collecting decisions and keep you motivated.

Navigating the Collector's Landscape

Your motivation for collecting will significantly influence how you navigate the numismatic landscape. Historical collectors might find themselves spending hours in antique shops or at auction houses specializing in ancient artifacts. Those focused on investment might prioritize establishing relationships with reputable coin dealers or subscribing to services that alert them to market trends and opportunities. Understanding where to look for coins is just as important as knowing what to look for.

As you move forward in your coin-collecting adventure, remember that each coin you choose to collect should resonate with your personal motivations and goals. Whether driven by the allure of history or the dynamics of investment, your collection will ultimately reflect your unique journey through the fascinating world of numismatics.

UNDERSTANDING COIN TERMINOLOGY

Navigating the realm of coin collecting can initially seem like learning a new language. Familiarity with key terms not only enhances your understanding but also boosts your confidence in participating in discussions, making purchases, or evaluating your collection. This glossary section is designed to demystify the terminology you'll frequently encounter, paving the way for a more informed and enjoyable collecting experience.

2005 Lincoln Penny

Let's start with the basics of coin anatomy. The 'obverse' of a coin is commonly called the "head" and usually features a prominent design or portrait, often including notable historical figures or symbolic imagery. For instance, the obverse of US quarters prominently displays the profile of George Washington. In contrast, the 'reverse', or "tail", typically showcases an emblem or a motif representing national identity, such as the bald eagle or state-specific designs seen on US state quarters. Understanding these terms helps immensely when reading descriptions in catalogs or discussing purchases with dealers.

Another critical aspect is the 'edge' of the coin, which can be plain, reeded (with grooves), or lettered.

Coin Edges - Plain, reeded and lettered.

Knowing the type of edge a coin has can sometimes help identify its authenticity, as some counterfeiters may overlook this detail. Lastly, the 'mint mark' is a small letter or symbol on a coin that indicates where the coin was minted. For example, a 'D' denotes the Denver Mint, and an 'S' signifies the San Francisco Mint. Collectors often seek coins from specific mints, especially if they are known for lower production runs, making the coins rarer and potentially more valuable.

Decoding the Grading Scale

Grading is crucial as it directly affects a coin's value. The scale ranges from 'Poor' (P-1), where the coin's details are barely recognizable, to 'Perfect Uncirculated' (MS-70), which indicates a mint condition without any signs of wear. Most coins fall somewhere in between. For instance, a coin graded 'Good' (G-4) shows significant wear but maintains the main designs, while 'Fine' (F-12) coins have lighter wear, and all considerable details are clear. 'Very Fine' (VF-20) coins show only light wear on the highest points of the design.

By understanding these grades, you can better assess the coins you're considering adding to your collection and their appropriate market value, ensuring you make informed decisions whether you're buying or selling.

Coin-Collecting Slang and Acronyms

As you delve deeper into the coin-collecting community, you'll encounter a variety of slang and acronyms. Terms like 'numismatics', which refers to the study or collection of currency, including coins, tokens, paper money, and related objects, are fundamental. Others, such as 'bag marks'—small nicks and scratches on coins caused by contact with other coins in a mint bag—are more niche but equally important to know. Acronyms such as 'BU' (Brilliant Uncirculated) describe a coin's condition and are essential when evaluating ungraded coins. Familiarity with these terms will not only help you in discussions and transactions but also deepen your connection with the broader community of collectors.

Transaction Terms

Finally, understanding transaction terms is critical to navigating purchases and sales effectively. Terms like 'bid', 'ask', and 'reserve' are commonplace in auctions. The 'bid' is the price a buyer is willing to pay, while the 'ask' is the lowest price the seller is willing to accept. A 'reserve' is a minimum price set by the seller, and if bidding does not reach this price, the item will not be sold. Knowing these terms ensures that when you participate in auctions, either in person or online, you do so with a clear understanding of the process, enhancing your chances of making successful transactions.

SETTING UP YOUR COIN COLLECTING SPACE

Creating an optimal environment for collecting and preserving coins is a fundamental step every enthusiast should consider seriously. Coins, especially those made from precious metals, are susceptible to a variety of environmental factors that can degrade their condition and diminish their value. Understanding how to store and handle your collection properly ensures that each piece retains its historical significance and market value for years to come.

Choosing the Right Environment

The ideal environment for storing coins is a space that is cool, dry, and stable. Fluctuations in temperature and humidity are among the biggest threats to coin preservation. High humidity can lead to corrosion and tarnishing, particularly for coins made from copper and silver, while excessive heat can accelerate these damaging reactions. Ideally, the room where you store your coins should have a temperature maintained between 65 and 70 degrees Fahrenheit with a relative humidity of around 50%. It's also wise to keep the storage area free from pollutants and chemicals, such as those found in common household cleaners, as these can cause further deterioration. For collectors living in areas with high humidity or fluctuating temperatures, investing in a climate-controlled cabinet or safe can be a prudent decision.

Storage Solutions

When considering storage solutions, the primary goal is to protect the coins from handling and environmental exposure while keeping them organized and accessible. Coin albums are a popular choice for many collectors as they allow for easy viewing and organization of the collection. These typically consist of pages with individual pockets made from soft, PVC-free plastic that won't scratch the coins. However, for particularly valuable or delicate coins, a more secure option might be preferable.

Coin capsules provide robust protection by enclosing each coin in an airtight container, usually made from acrylic or another inert material. These are particularly effective at shielding the coin from air and touch, thereby preventing oxidation and other forms of degradation. For the highest level of protection, especially for investment-grade coins, it might be worth considering high-quality, temperature-controlled safes or custom storage solutions that combine security with optimal environmental controls.

The choice between display-oriented solutions like albums and higher-protection options like capsules often depends on the individual collector's goals and the nature of their collection. Those who collect primarily for enjoyment may prefer albums for their ease of access and display qualities, whereas those who view their collection as an investment might opt for the security and preservation benefits of capsules and safes.

Master the Technique of Handling Coins

Proper handling is crucial to maintaining a coin's condition. The oils and acids present on human skin can leave permanent marks and corrosion on a coin's surface. Therefore, handling coins with clean cotton gloves is advisable to prevent direct contact with the skin. When you must handle coins without gloves, do so by their edges, avoiding touching the faces of the coins. This minimizes the risk of diminishing the coin's grade due to fingerprints or smudging, which is especially important for uncirculated or proof coins.

Additionally, always hold a coin over a soft surface, such as a padded tray or a velvet cloth. This way, if the coin is accidentally dropped, it lands on a soft surface, reducing the risk of dings or scratches. These precautions might seem minor, but they can significantly impact the long-term preservation and value of your collection.

Documentation and Cataloging

Keeping a detailed record of your coin collection is as crucial as physically preserving the coins. Documentation should include not only a description and photograph of each coin but also information about its provenance, purchase date, price, and any other relevant historical or valuation data. This record becomes invaluable for insurance purposes should your collection be damaged or stolen. Furthermore, should you decide to sell or trade part of your collection, potential buyers will likely require detailed information about the coins' condition and history.

For collectors who view their hobby as part of their legacy, proper documentation ensures that future generations understand the value and significance of each piece in the collection. Software and apps specifically designed for coin collectors can make the process of cataloging and managing a collection more straightforward and more efficient. These tools not only help in keeping track of your collection but can also provide insights into market values and trends, helping you make informed decisions about future acquisitions or sales.

By meticulously setting up the right environment, choosing suitable storage solutions, handling coins correctly, and keeping detailed records, you ensure that your coin collection remains in the best possible condition. This not only preserves the coins' aesthetic and historical value but also maximizes their potential financial worth, allowing you to fully enjoy every aspect of this engaging hobby.

HOW TO START WITHOUT BREAKING THE BANK

Developing a budget for your new hobby in coin collecting is akin to setting a foundation for a house; it's essential for ensuring stability and preventing future financial mishaps. As someone who values both the historical and potential investment aspects of collecting, aligning your financial resources with your collecting goals is crucial. Initial enthusiasm can quickly lead to overspending, particularly if you dive into purchasing without a clear plan. The key is to develop a budget that reflects your financial reality and collecting ambitions, allowing you to enjoy growing your collection without the stress of financial strain.

Crafting a Hobby Budget that Fits Your Finances

The first step in budgeting effectively is to assess your disposable income—what is available after essential expenses like housing, utilities, and groceries. From this, decide a percentage that feels comfortable to dedicate to coin collecting. This isn't just about buying coins; consider other costs like storage, accessories, and educational materials. It's also wise to set aside a part of this budget as a contingency fund for unexpected opportunities—a rare coin coming up for auction might demand a swift, decisive purchase. Remember, the goal of setting up a budget isn't to limit your enjoyment but to enhance it by removing financial uncertainty and potential regret from impulsive decisions.

Cost-Effective Collecting Strategies

One effective strategy to stretch your coin-collecting budget is to specialize in a particular niche. This could be a specific historical period, type of coin, or coins from a certain country. Niche collecting not only narrows your focus but also allows you to become more knowledgeable in that area, which can ensure good buying decisions. For example, specializing in pre-20th century American coins or British colonial coins can provide your collection with thematic coherence, potentially increasing its value both as a historical archive and a financial investment. Moreover, by focusing on a niche, you can more easily identify underpriced coins in your area of expertise, allowing for smarter investments that fit your budget.

Master Coin Valuation to Guide Your Purchases

Understanding the factors that influence coin values is crucial for making informed purchasing decisions. Rarity, demand, condition, and historical significance all play significant roles in determining a coin's value. Staying informed through regular research is essential; utilize resources like online databases, auction records, and numismatic publications to keep track of market trends and price fluctuations. This knowledge not only prevents overpaying but also helps in identifying the right time to purchase or sell, maximizing the potential return on investment. For instance, if you notice that coins from a particular era are beginning to increase in demand, you might decide to focus your acquisitions in that area, predicting further increases in value.

Invest in Knowledge for Informed Collecting

Lastly, investing in your numismatic education can yield dividends far greater than any single coin purchase. Spending part of your budget on quality resources—books, courses, seminars, and memberships to numismatic societies—can equip you with the knowledge to make wiser decisions and potentially avoid costly mistakes. For example, understanding the grading system used for coins can directly influence your purchasing decisions and ability to negotiate prices. Additionally, attending seminars and courses offers the opportunity to meet seasoned collectors and experts whose insights and experiences are invaluable. These educational investments ensure that your collecting strategy is built on a solid foundation of knowledge and expertise, ultimately enhancing both the enjoyment and the profitability of your hobby.

Incorporating these budgetary strategies will ensure that your venture into coin collecting is both financially sustainable and deeply rewarding. By aligning your financial resources with strategic purchasing and educational investments, you pave the way for a collection that not only satisfies your passion for history and investment but also stands as a testament to thoughtful and informed collecting.

CHAPTER TWO

IDENTIFYING YOUR COINS

As you delve deeper into the world of coin collecting, the ability to accurately identify and assess your coins becomes paramount. This chapter is designed to enhance your understanding of the physical aspects of coins, which are as rich in detail as they are in history. Here, you'll learn to not only recognize but also appreciate the intricate elements that make each coin unique and valuable. Whether examining a coin held in your hand or evaluating a potential acquisition, the knowledge you gain here will be indispensable.

THE ANATOMY OF A COIN

Every coin tells a story, not just through its imagery but also through its structure. The 'obverse' of a coin is typically what one might consider the 'front'. It often features a portrait or a national emblem that holds significance to the issuing country. This side of the coin usually includes the year of minting and, sometimes, key national symbols or the name of the figure depicted. The 'reverse', or the 'back' side of the coin, typically carries a motif or a design that pays tribute to the nation's culture, achievements, or landmarks.

Obverse and reverse 1977 Washington Quarter

For instance, U.S. quarters feature changing reverse designs that commemorate national parks and historic sites as part of the America the Beautiful series. Understanding these elements is crucial not just for appreciation but for authentication and valuation purposes as well.

The collectibility and value of a coin can be significantly influenced by its visual attributes, including its color, luster, and the presence of any distinctive markings. For example, the luster of a coin, which refers to its shine and reflective qualities, can indicate its condition and authenticity. Older coins might have a soft, satiny luster, while newer coins could display a more brilliant, mirror-like sheen. Additionally, features such as unusual colorations or double strikes can add to a coin's rarity and desirability among collectors.

Understand Mint Marks to Identify Coin Origins

Mint marks are tiny letters or symbols on coins that indicate where the coin was produced. For example, a coin minted in Denver, USA, bears a 'D' mark, while one from San Francisco bears an 'S'. These marks are usually found on the obverse of the coin, but their placement can vary depending on the specific coin and minting year. Collectors often seek coins from specific mints, especially those that are less common, as this can affect the coin's rarity and value. Understanding mint marks is essential for anyone looking to collect coins from specific mints or to complete a series that includes representations from all possible mints.

Identify variations and minting errors that impact coin value.

Coin variations and errors can occur during the minting process, leading to unique features that can be highly prized by collectors. These can range from double dies, where the details of a coin are mistakenly stamped twice by the coin press, to off-center strikes that give the coin an unusual appearance. For example, a 1955 double-die penny, where the obverse side has overlaid images due to misalignment during minting, is considered one of the most famous error coins and can fetch a significant sum.

1955 double-die penny

Recognizing these errors involves a keen eye and knowledge about what constitutes a 'normal' coin, making this skill invaluable for collectors who enjoy hunting for these rarities.

By mastering the anatomy of coins and understanding the significance of their various features, you equip yourself with the knowledge to make informed decisions about your collection. This chapter serves as your guide through the complex yet rewarding process of coin identification, paving the way for more advanced topics in coin collecting. As you continue to build your collection, keep these insights in mind— they are your tools for unlocking the stories and values held within each piece of your growing numismatic treasure.

UNDERSTANDING GLOBAL CURRENCY

The allure of coin collecting extends far beyond the borders of one's own country, embracing a diverse array of designs, metals, and histories from around the globe. Each coin, whether it comes from the bustling markets of India or the quiet mints of Switzerland, carries with it a piece of its national spirit and heritage. For collectors, understanding the global scope of numismatics opens up a vast field of opportunities and insights, not only into the world of finance but also into cultures and histories that may be vastly different from their own.

1959 sovereign with Queen Elizabeth II's portrait.

The diversity of world coins is astounding. Consider, for instance, the vivid history reflected in British sovereigns, which bear witness to an empire where the sun never set, or the intricate artistry of Japanese yen coins, which capture the aesthetic sensibilities of different eras in Japan's history.

1889 Japanese 1 yen coin featuring Emperor Meiji.

Then there are the peso coins of Mexico, each narrating stories of revolution and resilience. Such coins are not merely currency; they are miniature ambassadors of their countries' cultures and times. As a collector, when you hold a foreign coin, you hold a piece of the world, each with its unique tale and intrinsic charm.

1901 Mexican Un Peso featuring Liberty and "Republica Mexicana" inscription

For those looking to focus their collections, certain regions stand out due to the historical and monetary value of their coins. Europe, for example, is renowned for its centuries-old coins like the British Pound or the Swiss Franc, which are not only steeped in rich history but also hold considerable value in the collector's market. Asia offers unique finds like the Chinese Yuan, which dates back to the 19th century and features an array of dynastic symbols that are highly sought after by collectors.

Song-Yuan dynasty amulet coin, valued for its historical significance and intricate design.

Even the Pacific islands, though smaller in economic scale, produce fascinating coinage such as the Samoan tala, which often features exotic wildlife and natural beauty, reflecting the island's lush landscapes.

Navigating currency conversion is crucial when dealing with world coins. The value of foreign coins is often not immediately apparent, particularly when dealing with historical or antique specimens whose face values no longer reflect their market worth. Understanding the current exchange rates and the historical context of a coin's value requires a bit of research but is essential for making informed decisions. Tools like currency converters or financial apps can be invaluable here, helping you understand the real-time value of coins in your collection compared to your local currency. This knowledge not only aids in purchasing decisions but also helps in evaluating the potential return on investment for the coins you choose to collect.

Legal considerations also play a significant role when expanding your collection to include international coins. Different countries have various regulations regarding the export and import of historical and valuable coins. For instance, countries with rich cultural heritage, like Egypt and Greece, have strict laws to prevent the export of coins that are considered national treasures. Even within trade-friendly zones like the European Union, specific paperwork and declarations might be required to move coins across borders legally. It's advisable to consult legal experts or customs officials when planning to purchase significant pieces from abroad, ensuring that your additions are not just valuable but also compliant with international laws. This not only protects you legally but also ensures that the coins' provenance is preserved, maintaining their history and value for future generations.

By embracing the diverse world of global coinage, you open up a panorama of collecting opportunities. Each coin adds a layer to the rich tapestry of your collection, bringing with it a story of its own, a snippet of history, and a dash of international mystique. As you continue to explore the vast world of coins, remember that each piece you add not only enriches your collection but also deepens your connection with the world at large.

Revealing the Stories Behind Historical Coins

Coins are not merely pieces of metal used for transactions; they are snapshots of the epochs they originate from, encapsulating the historical, political, and social nuances of their time. Understanding coins as historical documents involves more than just recognizing their monetary value—it requires a deep appreciation of their roles in the annals of history. For instance, Roman coins often bore the likeness of the reigning emperor, serving as a tool for propaganda as well as currency, spreading the emperor's image throughout the empire and asserting his dominance and god-like status among the subjects. Similarly, during pivotal changes in regime or governmental shifts, new coins were often minted to reflect those changes, offering insights into shifts in power and policy.

This historical intimacy is not confined to ancient coins. Even more modern examples, like the American Buffalo nickel, tell stories of cultural significance and national identity. Minted in the early 20th century, this coin featured a Native American and an American bison, symbols that are deeply woven into the United States' historical fabric.

Buffalo Nickel (Type II): Native American profile on the obverse, American bison on the reverse, minted in 1913.

Each coin, through its imagery, composition, and circulation, can reveal much about the economic conditions, technological advancements, and cultural values of the period in which it was minted. Collectors, therefore, do not just collect coins; they collect pieces of history, each with a story to tell.

Coins are often celebrated not only for their age or rarity but also for their historical significance. Some coins have had pivotal roles in history, becoming famous beyond numismatic circles. The 1933 Double Eagle, for instance, is renowned for its rarity and the intriguing history it carries.

Saint-Gaudens Double Eagle (1907)

Originally minted during the Great Depression in the United States, most of these coins were melted down before they could enter circulation in an effort to stabilize the gold standard.

However, a few specimens escaped this fate and entered the collector's market under mysterious circumstances, making them some of the most sought-after—and storied—coins in the world. The tales of such coins often add an intangible value that transcends their material worth, making them highly prized possessions among collectors.

Deciphering Symbols and Inscriptions

The art of reading and interpreting the symbols and inscriptions on coins can be likened to deciphering a coded message from the past. Each symbol, and letter carries meaning and intent, and they are placed deliberately to convey specific messages or assert certain ideologies. For example, many ancient coins feature gods and goddesses, symbolizing the divine right of rulers or the protection of the state by higher powers. Inscriptions, often in Latin or Greek on older coins, might declare the ruler's titles, achievements, or intentions. Learning to decipher these messages requires not only an understanding of the language but also an awareness of the historical and cultural context in which the coin was minted.

For those interested in delving deeper into the symbols and inscriptions, it's beneficial to start with a focus on a specific era or region, gradually expanding your knowledge base. Resources such as numismatic reference books, academic papers, and even online databases can provide translations and explanations.

Additionally, engaging with fellow collectors and historians through forums or clubs can offer insights and aid in your understanding of these complex and fascinating aspects of coin collecting.

Researching Your Coins

The endeavor to uncover the full story behind a coin can be as thrilling as the initial discovery of the coin itself. Effective research strategies are essential for any collector aiming to deepen their understanding of their coins' backgrounds. Start by documenting every detail of the coin—its weight, diameter, design, and any markings or inscriptions. This initial cataloging is crucial as it helps in identifying the coin through databases or reference materials.

Utilizing a variety of sources enriches your research. Historical coin catalogs and numismatic books are invaluable for providing detailed descriptions and historical contexts. Online databases and auction sites offer insights into current valuations and recent discoveries in the field. Visiting museums or attending exhibitions can also provide contextual understanding and connections with experts in the field.

For a more hands-on approach, consider visiting historical sites or regions from which your coins originate when possible. Such visits can offer a tangible connection to the past and a better understanding of the coin's place within its original environment. Moreover, establishing relationships with reputable dealers and experienced collectors can provide opportunities for learning and even mentorship. These collectors often have specialized knowledge and can offer tips on both the finer points of coin analysis and the best research resources.

By treating each coin as a piece of history, you open up endless avenues for exploration and discovery. This approach does not just add depth to your collection but also enriches your experience as a collector, connecting you with centuries of human endeavor, culture, and artistry through the simple act of studying a coin. As you continue to build and explore your collection, remember that each coin, whether held in a museum or in your own collection, serves as a testament to the rich and varied narratives of our world's history.

IDENTIFYING MODERN COIN MINTS AND DESIGNS

The allure of modern coinage lies not only in its ability to act as legal tender but also in its role as a canvas for artistic and technological expression. Contemporary coin collecting opens a window into the modern advancements and cultural shifts that shape our societies today. Unlike their historical counterparts, modern coins often incorporate cutting-edge designs and manufacturing techniques, making them captivating both as collectibles and as snapshots of current innovation.

The appeal of current coin designs extends beyond mere aesthetics. Many modern mints use this opportunity to showcase national achievements, commemorate significant events, or highlight important cultural symbols. For instance, the recent series of coins might depict a groundbreaking scientific achievement or celebrate a national anniversary. These designs are not only appealing because of their freshness and relevance but also because they resonate on a personal level with collectors who have lived through the events commemorated.

Innovations in coinage technology have dramatically transformed the look and security features of coins. Modern mints now often employ laser etching, holographic elements, and colorization to enhance the visual appeal and the difficulty of counterfeiting. Bi-metallic coins, which use two different types of metals in one coin, are not only visually striking but also add a layer of complexity to the minting process that fascinates collectors. Additionally, some coins feature intricate micro-engravings that can only be seen under magnification, a testament to the precise artistry and advanced technology employed in their creation. These technological advancements make modern coins not just tools of trade but also marvels of engineering and design.

1999 Liberian $10 coin featuring a holographic Statue of Liberty.

Collecting commemorative coins is particularly popular among modern coin enthusiasts. These coins are usually issued to mark significant events or anniversaries and are often produced in limited quantities, which can enhance their value and appeal. The collectibility of such issues is also driven by their historical relevance and the emotional connection they can evoke. For example, a coin issued in remembrance of a national hero or a pivotal moment in history carries with it a weight that transcends its face value, making it a sought-after piece for any collection.

Speculating on which modern coins might become the classics of the future is an exciting aspect of collecting. Factors that make a coin a future classic include limited mintage, unique design elements, or coins that represent a 'first' in some way, such as the first use of a new minting technology or design feature. Coins that stir controversy, challenge artistic norms, or are part of a popular limited series may also gain prominence in the future. The potential for certain modern coins to appreciate in value or become key pieces in collections is considerable, adding an element of investment foresight to the hobby of collecting.

As we wrap up this exploration into modern coinage, it's clear that the dynamic nature of contemporary coins—rich in artistry, steeped in technology, and reflective of current times—makes them not only fascinating collectibles but also potential heirlooms of tomorrow. Their ability to capture the spirit of the age and their advanced security features make them standout candidates for the future classics of the numismatic world. By understanding the trends and innovations in modern minting, collectors are better equipped to appreciate and select pieces that might not only enrich their collections but also potentially appreciate in value over time.

Moving forward, the journey into coin grading awaits. As we transition from the art and innovation of modern minting to the precision of evaluating a coin's condition, the interconnectedness of these aspects becomes evident. Understanding the grade of a coin is crucial, not just for assessing its current worth but also for predicting its future value and appreciating its place within the broader narrative of numismatics.

CHAPTER THREE
COIN GRADING ESSENTIALS

Grading a coin is akin to uncovering layers of its life story; each mark, luster, and detail narrates its journey through time and commerce. As you delve into the realm of coin collecting, understanding how to grade a coin is paramount—it's the compass that guides collectors in navigating the vast seas of numismatics, especially when determining a coin's value and collectibility. Grading is not just a skill but an art form that, once mastered, can significantly enhance your appreciation and assessment of coins, turning your collecting into a more informed and rewarding experience.

Introduction to the Basics of Coin Grading

The grading scale for coins is a finely tuned system that evaluates a coin's condition from multiple aspects, including its mint state, wear, and overall appearance. This scale is crucial because the grade of a coin directly influences its market value

—the higher the grade, the more pristine the coin, and, typically, the higher its value. For instance, a coin graded as 'Fine' (F) shows considerable wear but retains full rims and major details, whereas a 'Mint State' (MS) coin exhibits no wear and appears just as it did when it left the mint.

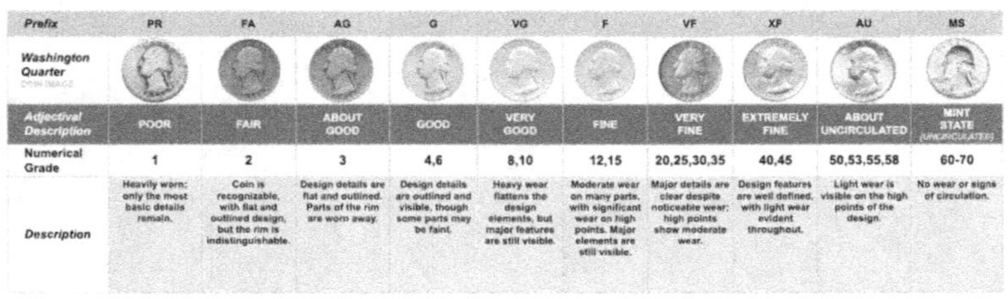

Prefix	PR	FA	AG	G	VG	F	VF	XF	AU	MS
Washington Quarter COIN IMAGE										
Adjectival Description	POOR	FAIR	ABOUT GOOD	GOOD	VERY GOOD	FINE	VERY FINE	EXTREMELY FINE	ABOUT UNCIRCULATED	MINT STATE (UNCIRCULATED)
Numerical Grade	1	2	3	4,6	8,10	12,15	20,25,30,35	40,45	50,53,55,58	60-70
Description	Heavily worn; only the most basic details remain.	Coin is recognizable, with flat and outlined design, but the rim is indistinguishable.	Design details are flat and outlined. Parts of the rim are worn away.	Design details are outlined and visible, though some parts may be faint.	Heavy wear flattens the design elements, but major features are still visible.	Moderate wear on many parts, with significant wear on high points. Major elements are still visible.	Major details are clear despite noticeable wear; high points show moderate wear.	Design features are well defined, with light wear evident throughout.	Light wear is visible on the high points of the design.	No wear or signs of circulation.

Navigating this scale requires a keen eye and an understanding of the nuances that differentiate one grade from another. Each grade reflects a specific range of qualities found in the coin's condition, from 'Poor' (P-1), where the coin is barely identifiable, to 'Mint State' (MS-70), which represents a flawless specimen as it would appear under 5x magnification. The subtleties that distinguish, for example, a 'Very Fine' (VF) from a 'Fine' (F) grade involve details such as the sharpness of the remaining design and the visibility of original mint luster.

The Impact of Condition on Value

The condition of a coin often holds the key to its past and its desirability. A higher-grade coin not only suggests a piece that has survived the years without significant wear but also one that potentially holds a greater historical or aesthetic value. Collectors prize such coins because they are rarer and often more visually appealing. For example, an 1885 Morgan Silver Dollar in a Mint State grade could fetch thousands of dollars at auction, significantly more than the same coin in a lower grade. This premium on higher-grade coins is driven by both their scarcity and the higher demand among collectors who seek the best specimens for their collections.

Visual Grading vs Technical Grading

Grading can be approached in two primary ways: visual and technical. Visual grading relies on the grader's overall impression of the coin's appearance, considering factors like luster, color, and eye appeal. This method, while somewhat subjective, is often used by collectors to make quick assessments. Technical grading, on the other hand, is a more detailed process that examines specific criteria such as strike quality, the presence of wear, and flaws like scratches or contact marks. This method often requires tools such as magnifying glasses or microscopes and is generally more precise and consistent.

Balancing these two approaches can provide a more holistic view of a coin's grade. While technical grading offers accuracy, visual grading accounts for the aesthetic aspects that might make a coin particularly desirable or unique despite technical flaws.

Common Grading Mistakes

New collectors often make several common mistakes when grading coins. One such error is overgrading, where the condition of a coin is assessed more favorably than it should be. This can happen due to a lack of experience or a misunderstanding of the grading standards. To avoid this, familiarize yourself with the grading criteria and compare coins to high-quality images of coins in similar grades. Another frequent mistake is failing to account for environmental damage, such as corrosion or cleaning, which can significantly lower a coin's grade and value.

Using consistent lighting and magnification can help mitigate these errors, providing a stable environment to assess each coin accurately. Additionally, participating in grading workshops or working with more experienced collectors can provide practical insights and feedback, helping you refine your grading skills over time.

Grading is not just about placing a coin into a category; it's about understanding its past, its rarity, and its beauty. As you continue to explore the chapters of this book, remember that each coin you grade adds to your experience, enhancing not just your collection but also your journey in the fascinating world of numismatics.

GRADING SYSTEMS

The Sheldon Scale, developed by Dr. William Sheldon in 1949, originally served to grade large cents but has since been universally adopted across various coin types. This numerical system ranges from 1 to 70, where 1 represents a barely identifiable coin, and 70 denotes a flawless specimen. The scale is structured to reflect the condition of a coin with numerical precision, providing a more objective measure that helps collectors and dealers alike assess a coin's value.

Number	Grade
1	Basal State-1
2	Fair
3	Very Fair
4, 5, 6	Good
7, 8, 10	Very Good
12, 15	Fine
20, 30	Very Fine
40	Extremely Fine
50	About Uncirculated
60	Mint State
65	Mint State
70	Mint State

The Sheldon Grading System

For example, coins graded from 60 to 70 are considered uncirculated, meaning they show no signs of wear because they haven't been used in commerce. The higher the number within this range, the fewer the imperfections. A grade of 70, which is rare, indicates a coin that has maintained its mint state perfection with full original luster and no signs of handling or wear. This precision in grading allows collectors to assess not just the beauty and preservation of a coin but also its potential market value, making the Sheldon Scale a critical tool in the numismatic field.

The application of the Sheldon Scale requires a detailed examination of the coin's surface, assessing aspects like luster, color, and strike quality, alongside noting any detracting marks or wear. This methodical approach ensures that each coin is evaluated on a consistent basis, providing a reliable framework for comparison across collections and sales platforms. It's essential for you, as a collector, to familiarize yourself with this scale because understanding it can significantly enhance your ability to participate knowledgeably in the buying and selling of coins.

Alternative Grading Systems

While the Sheldon Scale is widely recognized, several alternative grading systems also exist and can be particularly useful depending on the type of coins you are collecting. For instance, the European Grading System, which uses terms like Good, Very Good, Fine, Very Fine, and Extremely Fine, is commonly employed in European countries and may be encountered when dealing with international transactions or collections. This system focuses more on descriptive categories rather than a precise numerical scale, providing a broader assessment of a coin's condition.

Another notable system is the ANA (American Numismatic Association) Standards, which include a detailed set of guidelines for grading U.S. coins. This system is often used in conjunction with the Sheldon Scale in the United States to provide a more comprehensive understanding of a coin's condition. It includes criteria for evaluating the strike of the coin, the presence of any wear, and other factors that could affect its overall grade. Understanding these alternative systems is beneficial when dealing with diverse collections or when engaging in international trade, as it broadens your ability to assess and communicate about coins accurately.

Professional Grading Services

Professional grading services play a pivotal role in the coin-collecting ecosystem. Entities such as the Numismatic Guaranty

Corporation (NGC) and Professional Coin Grading Service (PCGS) offer expert grading services that provide a reliable third-party assessment of a coin's condition. These services employ seasoned experts who use advanced tools to grade coins, ensuring a high level of accuracy and consistency. The grades assigned by these services are recognized internationally and can significantly impact a coin's marketability and value.

Utilizing professional grading services can be especially beneficial when dealing with high-value coins where the grade could substantially influence the selling price. These services also encapsulate graded coins in sealed holders that preserve their condition and authenticate the grade, which can enhance buyer confidence and streamline sales processes. For collectors, the assurance that comes with a professionally graded coin can justify the cost of grading, especially in transactions involving rare or highly valuable pieces.

Interpreting Grading Certificates

Grading certificates, often provided by professional grading services, are documents that authenticate a coin's grade and condition. These certificates typically include detailed information about the coin, such as its year of mintage, denomination, and the specifics of its condition that led to its grade. Understanding how to read these certificates is crucial for you as it enables you to verify the coin's assessed value and ensures transparency in transactions.

A typical grading certificate will list the coin's grade at the top, followed by descriptors of its visual appeal and any notable flaws. It may also include a certification number, which can be used to verify the coin's grading information in the service's online database. This number acts as a safeguard against counterfeiting of the certificate and provides a traceable record of the coin's evaluation. By learning to interpret these documents, you can confidently assess the value of graded coins and make informed decisions in your collecting and investment endeavors.

DIY COIN GRADING

When you're ready to take the plunge into grading your coins, having the right tools at your disposal can make a significant difference in accuracy and ease. Essential tools for any aspiring coin grader include a high-quality magnifying glass or a jeweler's loupe, which typically offers magnification from 5x to 10x. This tool is crucial for closely examining the finer details of a coin's surface, such as mint marks, minor scratches, or the subtleties of its relief. Another indispensable tool is a good light source. A daylight-balanced lamp can help illuminate the coin's actual color and surface details without the distortion caused by typical household lighting.

Digital calipers are also beneficial, especially for verifying the dimensions of a coin, which can be critical when determining authenticity or detecting irregularities. For more advanced graders, a microscope might be used to inspect extremely fine details or to confirm suspicions of alterations or damage that aren't visible to the naked eye. Lastly, consider having a soft, lint-free cloth for handling coins, reducing the risk of adding new fingerprints or smudges, and a padded tray to provide a safe surface on which to place the coins during examination.

Setting up a dedicated grading area in your home can further enhance your grading activities. Ensure this space is free from potential contaminants like food, drinks, or oily substances, and maintain a well-organized and clean environment to protect the coins from accidental damage.

Grading coins at home begins with a thorough visual inspection. Start by examining the coin's obverse (front) and reverse (back) under your magnifying tool. Look for any signs of wear, especially on the highest points of the design, which are the first to show wear. Assess the luster; an uncirculated coin should still have a mint luster that appears as a sort of shine that radiates from the surface when the coin is moved under a light source. Check for any scratches, dents, or marks that could impact the coin's grade.

Next, inspect the edge of the coin for any irregularities or damage, as the edge can often be overlooked. After the visual inspection, measure the coin's diameter and thickness with your calipers to ensure the specifications match those typical for the coin, as discrepancies can indicate counterfeits or alterations.

Document your findings for each coin, making notes about every aspect of your inspection. This record will not only help you track the condition of your own collection but will also be invaluable if you decide to sell or have the coin professionally graded in the future.

Practicing Your Grading Skills

Improving your coin grading skills is a gradual process that benefits immensely from practice and patience. One effective way to hone your skills is to compare your graded coins with examples from trusted sources, such as professional grading services or established numismatic collections. This comparison can give you a more concrete idea of how professional graders assess and categorize coins, which can refine your grading criteria.

Participating in coin-collecting forums and communities can also be incredibly beneficial. Many collectors are happy to share their knowledge and may offer constructive feedback on your grading assessments. Attend local or national coin shows whenever possible; these events often offer seminars or workshops on coin grading, and they provide a chance to see a wide variety of coins and learn from experienced collectors and dealers.

Another practical method to enhance your grading accuracy is to use a grading checklist that includes all the factors you need to consider, such as luster, marks, wear, and strike. This checklist can ensure you don't overlook any aspects during the grading process.

LEARNING TO TRUST YOUR JUDGMENT

As you grow more accustomed to grading coins, trusting your judgment becomes crucial. Confidence in grading often develops from continued learning and hands-on experience, so immerse yourself regularly in grading exercises and stay updated with grading standards and techniques. However, it's also important to recognize the limits of DIY grading. While you can assess many aspects of a coin's condition at home, some scenarios, such as verifying the authenticity of a highly valuable coin or detecting sophisticated counterfeits, require the expertise and equipment of professional grading services.

In such cases, don't hesitate to seek out professional opinions. Remember, the goal of DIY grading isn't just to determine the value of your coins but also to enjoy and deepen your engagement with the hobby of coin collecting. By approaching grading with a balance of confidence and caution, you ensure that the process remains both rewarding and accurate, fostering a collection that truly reflects both your dedication and your passion for numismatics.

When to Seek Professional Grading

In the nuanced world of coin collecting, the decision to seek professional grading can sometimes feel as weighty as the coins themselves. Recognizing when to turn to the experts is crucial, especially when the stakes involve significant financial investment or historical importance. Typically, professional grading is advisable when dealing with rare or potentially high-value coins where the grade could substantially impact their market value. For instance, if you come across an old coin that you suspect might be of considerable value, having it professionally graded could not only confirm its condition but also enhance its credibility and salability in the market.

Professional grading becomes particularly important in scenarios where the authenticity of a coin is in question. Counterfeits and replicas can sometimes be so convincing that only a trained eye equipped with advanced technological tools can discern their true nature. Additionally, if you're planning to sell a part of your collection, professionally graded coins often fetch higher prices, as they come with a guarantee of their condition and authenticity. This is especially true in online markets, where buyers rely heavily on grading certificates to make purchasing decisions.

Choosing the right grading service is another essential step in the process. Look for services that are widely recognized and accredited, such as the Numismatic Guaranty Corporation (NGC) or the Professional Coin Grading Service (PCGS). These organizations have established a strong reputation for accuracy, consistency, and integrity in grading. Before sending a coin for grading, research the service's grading standards, turnaround times, and fee structures. It's also advisable to check reviews or ask for recommendations from other collectors to ensure that the service's standards align with your expectations.

Understanding the costs involved in professional grading is also important. Grading fees generally depend on the type of service chosen and the value of the coin. For example, standard grading services charge a fee based on the declared value of the coin, while more comprehensive services that include authentication and high-resolution imaging might cost more. However, the investment in professional grading can be worthwhile, particularly if it significantly enhances the coin's value or if it helps in making a more informed decision about purchasing or selling a coin.

Maximizing the value of your coins through professional grading is not just about achieving a higher sale price. It's also about the peace of mind that comes from knowing the true condition of your coins. Professionally graded coins are sealed in tamper-proof holders with a label displaying the grade, which preserves the coin's condition and prevents any future handling damage. This not only maintains the coin's aesthetic appeal but also its historical integrity, making it more attractive to potential buyers or as a treasured addition to a collection.

In conclusion, professional grading is a critical tool in the arsenal of any serious coin collector. It provides an authoritative assessment of a coin's condition, enhances its marketability, and helps maintain its condition over time. As you move forward in your collecting journey, understanding when and how to use professional grading services will undoubtedly refine your approach to collecting and investing in coins, paving the way for more informed and successful numismatic endeavors.

As the curtain falls on the complexities of coin grading, we transition to understanding another crucial aspect of numismatics—spotting and avoiding counterfeit coins. This next chapter will equip you with the knowledge to protect your investments and ensure that your collection remains as authentic as it is valuable.

CHAPTER FOUR

SPOTTING AND AVOIDING COUNTERFEITS

As you delve deeper into the world of coin collecting, understanding the authenticity of each piece becomes paramount. Imagine the thrill of discovering what appears to be a rare, vintage coin, only to realize it's a cleverly crafted counterfeit. Such experiences are not just disappointing but can also be financially detrimental. That's why becoming adept at spotting and avoiding fakes is as crucial as recognizing a genuine treasure. This chapter will guide you through the murky waters of counterfeit coins, equipping you with the knowledge to safeguard your precious collection.

COMMON TECHNIQUES IN COIN COUNTERFEITING

Counterfeiting has been an unfortunate aspect of numismatics since coins were first minted. Modern counterfeiters use a variety of sophisticated techniques to create fakes that can sometimes fool even the seasoned collector. Two common methods are casting and striking. Casting involves pouring molten metal into molds made from genuine coins. While this method can replicate the design, cast coins often exhibit telltale signs such as a lack of sharp detail, porous surfaces, and seam lines where the mold halves meet.

Striking, on the other hand, uses presses and dies to stamp out coins, similar to how legitimate mints produce them. Struck counterfeits can be more challenging to identify because they often better replicate the details and textures of genuine coins. However, discrepancies in the metal composition, weight, and sound (ring test) can sometimes give them away. Both methods require a discerning eye to spot irregularities, emphasizing the need for meticulous examination when assessing a coin's authenticity.

Detecting Telltale Signs

One of the first steps in detecting a counterfeit coin is checking its weight against the standard specifications for its type. Most genuine coins have a precise weight that counterfeiters often struggle to match exactly, especially if they use different metals or alloys. A high-precision scale is an invaluable tool in your collector's kit for this purpose.

Additionally, examine the coin's details under magnification. Look for inconsistencies in the artwork, text, or symbols that deviate from genuine specimens. Many counterfeit coins will have soft, mushy details or incorrect fonts due to the limitations of the counterfeiting process. Edges and border details should also be inspected; many genuine coins have specific patterns or reeded edges that are difficult for counterfeiters to replicate perfectly.

Historical vs. Modern Counterfeits

Historically, counterfeiting methods were often less sophisticated but could still pose significant challenges to authorities and collectors. Ancient counterfeiters commonly shaved off small amounts of precious metals from genuine coins to create new ones, a practice known as clipping. They would also frequently cover cheaper base metals with thin layers of silver or gold, a technique known as plating.

Modern counterfeiters have access to advanced technologies that can produce fakes with a high degree of accuracy. They use modern machining, electroplating, and even laser etching, which can sometimes replicate the appearance of genuine minting techniques. However, modern analytical tools have also become more sophisticated, allowing collectors to detect even the most advanced fakes using methods such as X-ray fluorescence (XRF) analysis, which can non-destructively determine the elemental composition of a coin.

PROTECTING YOUR COLLECTION

Protecting your collection from counterfeits starts with education. Familiarize yourself with the coins you collect, understanding their physical characteristics, history, and common issues. Purchasing coins from reputable dealers who offer guarantees of authenticity can also significantly reduce the risk of acquiring counterfeit pieces. Many dealers belong to professional organizations that require adherence to ethical standards, providing an additional layer of security.

Another effective strategy is to use protective measures such as encapsulation. Encapsulating coins in tamper-proof slabs by reputable grading services not only preserves their condition but also assures future buyers of their authenticity. This is particularly important for high-value coins, where the provenance and certification can significantly impact their market value and desirability.

By developing a keen eye for detail and building a network of trusted sources, you can effectively shield your collection from the pitfalls of counterfeits. Remember, the integrity of your collection hinges not just on the historical and monetary value of the pieces but also on the confidence in their authenticity. Each step you take in learning to identify and avoid fakes is a step toward ensuring that your collection remains both valuable and respected in the numismatic community.

Digital Tools for Identifying Fake Coins

In your quest to maintain the integrity of your coin collection, embracing modern technology can be a game-changer. The advent of digital tools specifically designed for coin collectors has revolutionized the way we approach the authentication of coins. Digital magnifiers, for example, have become far more advanced than the simple magnifying glasses used in the past. These devices now offer features such as adjustable magnification settings, high-resolution imaging, and even the ability to capture and analyze images on a connected computer or smartphone. This technological leap allows collectors to examine coins with unprecedented clarity and detail, making it easier to spot inconsistencies and anomalies that could indicate counterfeiting.

Apart from hardware, numerous apps and websites have been developed to aid collectors in verifying the authenticity of their coins. These platforms often utilize vast databases of coin images and details to offer instant comparisons. Some apps also incorporate features like image recognition software, which can automatically compare your coin to known authentic examples and highlight potential discrepancies. This kind of technology not only saves time but also increases the accuracy of your assessments, allowing for a more confident approach to collecting.

Online Databases and forums for Authenticity Verification

The internet is a treasure trove of resources when it comes to coin collecting. Numerous online databases exist that catalog detailed information about almost every type of coin ever minted. These databases often include high-quality images and lists of known variants, errors, and, importantly, common counterfeits. By comparing a coin in your possession with these verified entries, you can glean insights into its authenticity. Websites like the Numismatic Guaranty Corporation (NGC) or Professional Coin Grading Service (PCGS) provide comprehensive databases and also offer services where you can check if a particular coin has been graded and authenticated.

Moreover, online forums and discussion boards are invaluable resources. These platforms allow you to connect with other collectors and experts who can offer advice and second opinions on the authenticity of coins. Engaging in these communities not only helps verify coins but also helps gain deeper insights and knowledge from experienced collectors. When using online forums, ensure that clear and detailed images of your coins are provided from multiple angles to facilitate accurate assessments from other members.

AI's Role in Identifying Counterfeit Coins

Artificial intelligence (AI) is beginning to play a significant role in the numismatics field, particularly in the identification of counterfeit coins. AI systems are trained using thousands of images of both genuine and counterfeit coins, learning subtle differences that may not be immediately obvious to even experienced collectors. These systems can analyze coins based on patterns, metal composition, wear, and other characteristics with a level of precision and speed unattainable by human experts alone.

The deployment of AI in coin authentication offers a promising boost in the fight against counterfeits. Some AI applications can now scan a coin and compare it to their database in real-time, providing a report on its likely authenticity along with reasons for that determination. This can be incredibly useful for collectors who deal with a high volume of coins or who encounter particularly sophisticated counterfeits. As AI technology continues to evolve, it will undoubtedly become a staple tool in the numismatist's arsenal.

USING DIGITAL TOOLS IN AUTHENTICITY CHECKS

To effectively utilize digital tools in coin authentication, start by ensuring that you have the appropriate setup. Invest in a high-quality digital magnifier or a smartphone with a good camera, as clear images are crucial for accurate analysis. When using image comparison software or apps, make sure that the lighting is consistent and that the coin is free from any obstructions like dust or fingerprints, which can skew the results.

Always update your apps and software regularly to benefit from the latest features and the most up-to-date databases. Additionally, while AI and digital tools offer powerful support, they should not be used in isolation. Combine these technological solutions with traditional methods of authentication, such as physical examination and consultation with other experts, to ensure a comprehensive approach to verifying the authenticity of your coins.

By embracing these digital advancements, you empower yourself to protect your collection with greater confidence and precision. As technology continues to evolve, staying informed and adaptable will help you maintain the authenticity and value of your numismatic collection.

LEARNING FROM COUNTERFEIT CASE STUDIES

In the intricate world of numismatics, every counterfeit coin that slips through detection teaches a valuable lesson. Consider the infamous case of the 1909-S VDB Lincoln Penny. Known for its rarity, this coin has been a prime target for counterfeiters. A well-documented incident involved a counterfeit coin that was sold at a major auction. The coin had been altered from a less rare 1909 VDB penny by adding the 'S' mintmark. Although the alteration was expertly done, subtle discrepancies in the alignment and depth of the mintmark raised suspicions among sharp-eyed collectors. The lesson here is clear: even the smallest details can reveal a forgery, emphasizing the importance of meticulous examination and familiarity with the authentic minting characteristics of rare coins.

Another enlightening example is the 1913 Liberty Head Nickel. Only five genuine pieces are known to exist, making them exceedingly rare and valuable. Counterfeit versions often surface in the market, created by altering lesser-value nickels from other years. One such counterfeit was identified when experts noticed that the weight and dimensions slightly deviated from those known for genuine 1913 Liberty Head Nickels. This incident underscores the importance of using precise tools to measure and compare every potential acquisition against verified specifications.

Avoiding Coin Authentication Failures

Mistaken authentication often occurs due to a combination of sophisticated counterfeiting techniques and occasional lapses in the vigilance of collectors and experts. A notable instance involved a series of counterfeit Morgan Dollars, which were mistakenly authenticated by several experienced collectors. These fakes were produced using sophisticated die-struck methods that closely mimicked the minting process, making them particularly convincing. The error was eventually discovered through metallurgical analysis, which revealed inconsistencies in the metal composition compared to genuine Morgan Dollars. This case highlights the critical role of incorporating scientific testing in the authentication process, particularly for coins that are highly susceptible to counterfeiting.

In another instance, a collection of ancient Roman coins was authenticated and sold to various collectors over several years before being discovered as modern forgeries. The forgeries were initially convincing due to their high-quality craftsmanship and patina that mimicked centuries of aging. It was only when a historian noticed anachronistic details in the coin designs that the truth came to light. This emphasizes the necessity of historical as well as physical verification, showcasing how a deep understanding of the historical context can be just as crucial as the physical examination of the coin itself.

Counterfeit Detection Success Stories and Techniques

Success in identifying counterfeit coins often stems from a combination of keen observation, technical knowledge, and, sometimes, intuition. A success story that stands out involves a collector at a small regional coin show who suspected a series of gold coins were counterfeit. By using a portable electronic gold tester, the collector was able to determine that the coins, although appearing genuine in design and wear, did not have the correct electrical conductivity properties of gold. This proactive use of technology not only prevented a costly mistake but also alerted the community to the presence of these sophisticated fakes.

Another collector was able to identify counterfeit 18th-century colonial coins by noticing inconsistencies in the aging process. The coins had a forced patina that looked uneven and superficial upon closer inspection under UV light, which revealed newer metal beneath. This collector's familiarity with the aging process of metals and the application of UV light examination provided a non-destructive method to confirm suspicions, showcasing an innovative approach to coin authentication.

Enhancing Skills in Spotting Fakes

Each counterfeit coin detected and each mistake made provides invaluable lessons that enrich the collector's expertise. The educational value of these experiences cannot be overstated, as they continually refine the methods and techniques used by collectors to authenticate coins. Engaging with these case studies, sharing experiences in numismatic circles, and learning from the missteps of others build a collective knowledge base that strengthens the entire collecting community.

By studying past counterfeiting cases and remaining vigilant about potential forgeries, collectors not only protect their own investments but also contribute to the integrity of numismatics as a discipline. It is through these meticulous practices and shared learning experiences that the hobby of coin collecting continues to thrive, preserving its historical significance and economic value for future generations.

Building a Support Network for Authenticity Verification

Navigating the complexities of coin collecting, especially when it comes to ensuring the authenticity of each coin, underscores the importance of having a robust support system. Building relationships with experienced collectors and experts can provide you with a reservoir of knowledge and a safety net when doubts about a coin's authenticity arise. These relationships are often forged through shared interests and can lead to mutual benefits, including the exchange of valuable insights and the strengthening of your own collecting acumen.

Creating a support system involves more than just making connections; it requires engaging actively with the community. This can be achieved by participating in coin shows, auctions, and especially coin clubs. Coin clubs are invaluable resources because they not only offer access to experienced collectors who are often eager to share their knowledge but also provide a platform for learning through workshops, talks, and hands-on sessions. These clubs often have a diverse membership, ranging from novices to seasoned experts, and the collaborative atmosphere can be incredibly enriching. When you bring a coin to a club meeting expressing doubts about its authenticity, the collective wisdom of the group can offer perspectives that you might have yet to consider. Moreover, the tactile experience of handling numerous coins at such gatherings deepens your understanding and sharpens your eye for detail.

In addition to leveraging informal community networks, engaging with professional numismatic organizations can elevate your understanding and capabilities in verifying coin authenticity. These organizations, such as the American Numismatic Association (ANA) or the Royal Numismatic Society (RNS), are pillars of the numismatic community, providing resources, education, and standards for ethical collecting. Membership in these organizations often comes with access to a wealth of resources, including libraries, lectures, and publications that are specifically geared toward education in the field of numismatics. Furthermore, these organizations adhere to strict guidelines for trading and authenticity verification, offering a layer of security and trust when purchasing or verifying coins.

When doubts about a coin's authenticity are particularly challenging or when a significant investment is at stake, it may be prudent to turn to trusted verification services. Services like the Numismatic Guaranty Corporation (NGC) or the Professional Coin Grading Service (PCGS) offer professional authentication and grading services that are recognized globally. Engaging with these services typically involves submitting the coin for a detailed examination, after which it is graded and, if authentic, encapsulated in a tamper-proof holder with a certification label. This not only confirms the coin's authenticity but also generally enhances its value and saleability. To engage effectively with these services, ensure that you understand their submission guidelines, fee structures, and the scope of their examination. This ensures that you are well-informed about what to expect from the process and can make the most out of their services.

Navigating the authenticity of coins requires a balanced approach that combines personal expertise with the collective knowledge and resources of the numismatic community. By building strong relationships within this community, leveraging the educational opportunities provided by professional organizations, and utilizing trusted verification services, you equip yourself with a comprehensive toolkit for authenticating your collection. This approach not only protects your investment but also enriches your experience as a collector, deepening your understanding of numismatics and enhancing your enjoyment of this enriching hobby.

As we close this chapter on identifying and avoiding counterfeits, we move forward with the confidence that comes from knowing how to protect our investments and deepen our engagement with the numismatic community. The next chapter will explore the fascinating world of preserving your coin collection, ensuring that each piece remains as impeccable as the day it was minted or discovered. This journey into preservation is not just about maintaining value; it's about respecting the history and artistry that each coin represents, securing a legacy that can be cherished for generations to come.

CHAPTER FIVE

THE HISTORICAL SIGNIFICANCE OF COINS

Imagine holding a piece of history in your hands—a coin that has been passed through countless fingers over centuries, each exchange a silent witness to the ebb and flow of human endeavors. Coins are not merely tools of commerce; they are storied artifacts that chronicle the tale of human civilization. In this chapter, we will explore the rich tapestry of coinage history, from its inception to the modern day, and uncover how these metallic storytellers have mirrored the societies that minted them.

COINS THROUGH THE AGES

The journey of coinage begins in the ancient kingdom of Lydia, around 600 BC, where the first known coins were minted. These early coins were made from electrum, a natural alloy of gold and silver, and marked the beginning of standardized currency. The concept quickly spread to ancient Greece, where cities began to mint their own coins, featuring distinctive designs that expressed their identity and values.

As we move through the timeline, the Roman Empire adopted coinage as a vital tool for trade and administration, introducing a range of gold, silver, and bronze denominations. The fall of Rome did not hinder the evolution of coinage; it merely shifted the centers of minting to the Byzantine Empire and later to the Islamic caliphates, where the art of coinage was refined further.

The Middle Ages saw the proliferation of coinage across Europe, with each feudal lord minting his own money. By the Renaissance, the advent of powerful city-states and the rise of powerful banking families in places like Florence and Venice saw the introduction of iconic coins such as the Florin and the Ducat, which were trusted well beyond their borders for their consistent gold content.

The Age of Discovery broadened the world of coinage as European empires minted vast quantities of coins to facilitate trade in their expanding territories. The Spanish pieces of eight, minted in the New World, became the world's first global currency, acceptable from the Americas to Asia.

Evolution of Coinage

Initially, coins were simple lumps of metal stamped with a mark of authority. However, as minting technology evolved, so did the complexity and beauty of coin designs. The Greeks began portraying their gods and heroes on their coins, turning each piece into a work of art. The Romans introduced portraits of their emperors, using coins as a medium for propaganda and a tool for solidifying the ruler's image across the empire.

The Middle Ages saw a regression in the quality of coin designs due to the decentralized nature of minting. However, the Renaissance revived the artistry of coins, with detailed portraits and intricate heraldic designs becoming common. The Industrial Revolution brought steam-powered coin presses, which increased the uniformity and intricacy of coins dramatically.

In modern times, coins have become canvases for national expression, featuring symbolic designs that reflect a country's history, culture, and values. The materials used have also diversified from the traditional silver and gold to include base metals and, more recently, polymer and bi-metallic coins, reflecting both economic needs and technological advancements.

Coins often evolve in response to historical events. For example, the economic turmoil of the post-Roman Empire saw the debasement of coinage, where coins contained less and less precious metal, reflecting the declining fortunes of the era. Conversely, the discovery of vast silver mines in Bolivia in the 16th century led to a boom in coin production, which fueled Spain's global ambitions and widespread inflation, known as the 'Price Revolution'.

Wars have also had a profound impact on coinage. During the Napoleonic Wars, many European nations resorted to minting lower-quality copper coins as gold and silver became scarce. In more modern times, during World War II, metals like copper and nickel were needed for the war effort, leading the United States and other countries to mint coins in alternative materials like steel.

Milestones in Numismatics

The study of coins, or numismatics, has its own set of milestones that have shaped our understanding of history. The Renaissance, which fostered a renewed interest in the classical cultures of Greece and Rome, also rekindled the scholarly study of ancient coins. This period saw the collection of coins emerge as a systematic pursuit, which helped historians piece together chronological details of past civilizations that were otherwise not recorded.

The 19th century introduced cataloging and more scientific approaches to numismatics, significantly aided by the advent of photography, which allowed for better sharing and study of coin designs and details. More recently, the digital age has transformed numismatics through the creation of extensive online databases and the use of advanced metallurgical analysis techniques. These tools have not only democratized access to the study of coins but have also helped authenticate ancient coins and understand their composition.

As we delve deeper into the history and significance of these metallic artifacts, remember that each coin you hold is not just a piece of metal—it's a piece of history shaped by the hands of time and the fortunes of empires. It tells a story of economic shifts, artistic endeavors, and human ingenuity—a story that continues to unfold with each new discovery in the field of numismatics. As collectors, we are not just guardians of wealth; we are keepers of history, each coin a chapter, each collection a saga of the human journey through the ages.

ICONIC COINS AND THEIR STORIES

Among the pantheon of numismatic treasures, few rival the mystique and allure of the 1933 Saint-Gaudens Double Eagle. This $20 gold coin, minted during the depths of the Great Depression, represents a poignant intersection of beauty and controversy. Originally struck as a regular issue coin, the entire mintage was ordered to be melted down after the United States went off the gold standard, making private ownership of gold certificates, bullion, and coins illegal.

However, a handful of these coins escaped the smelter's fire through various means, mostly illicit. Today, they are among the most coveted of all collector's items. One such coin sold at auction in 2021 for a staggering $18.9 million, showcasing not only its rarity but the intense fascination it commands. The surviving examples are mainly housed in secure locations, such as the Smithsonian Institution, ensuring their preservation and public accessibility while highlighting their storied past.

Another legendary discovery that captivates the imagination of collectors worldwide is the Saddle Ridge Hoard. Unearthed in 2013 by a couple walking their dog in California, this cache of over 1,400 gold coins from the 19th century, buried in decaying metal cans, represents one of the most significant finds of buried treasure in U.S. history. Valued at over $10 million, the coins range from $5 to $20 pieces and are believed to have been buried in the late 1800s. Theories about their origin abound, but no conclusive evidence has yet surfaced, adding an intriguing layer of mystery. These coins have been gradually sold, with some retained by the finders as a tangible link to a bygone era of American history.

Design Milestones

The realm of coin design is replete with artistic milestones that have elevated the craft to new heights. A prime example is the Australian Kangaroo gold bullion coin series, which features an annually changing design of one of Australia's most iconic animals. Introduced in 1989 by the Royal Australian Mint, these coins not only serve as legal tender but also as a canvas for showcasing the artistry and innovation in coin design. The intricate portrayals of kangaroos in dynamic poses not only capture the essence of the Australian outback but also reflect advancements in minting technology, including high-relief designs and laser etching that enhances detail and depth.

Another significant design innovation is found in the Canadian Maple Leaf coin. First issued in 1979 by the Royal Canadian Mint, this coin featured an advanced anti-counterfeiting measure known as Bullion DNA anti-counterfeiting technology. It includes a micro-engraved laser mark visible only under magnification, setting a new standard in the security and intricacy of coin design. The Maple Leaf coins are celebrated not only for their purity and legal tender status but also for their aesthetic appeal and the groundbreaking security features they incorporate.

Coins of Controversy

Coins often become embroiled in controversies that underscore their more than monetary value, serving as focal points for broader societal debates. The 2001 Alabama state quarter is one such example. Part of the U.S. Mint's 50 State Quarters Program, this coin featured Helen Keller with her name written in English and in braille, marking the first time braille was used on a circulating U.S. coin. However, its inclusion sparked debate among various advocacy groups and the public concerning the portrayal and the practicality of braille on such a small surface, highlighting ongoing discussions about accessibility and representation.

Similarly, the 1986 France 100 Franc coin, which depicted Marianne, a national symbol of the French Republic, in a modernized form with her cap pulled back, stirred public debate. Critics argued that the portrayal lacked the traditional, revolutionary spirit associated with Marianne, sparking discussions on national identity and the role of imagery in public memory. This coin serves as a reminder of how designs can become arenas for ideological struggle and national reflection.

Collector's Favorites

Certain coins capture the hearts of collectors not just for their rarity or value but for their stories and the cultural epochs they represent. The Morgan Silver Dollar, minted from 1878 to 1921 in the United States, is one such coin that has consistently captivated collectors. Named after its designer, George T. Morgan, this coin epitomizes the American spirit of the late 19th and early 20th centuries, symbolizing the nation's westward expansion and industrial growth. Its substantial silver content, large format, and distinctive design featuring Lady Liberty make it a favorite among collectors who see it as a tangible piece of American history and nostalgia.

Similarly, the British Gold Sovereign holds a special place in many collections due to its extensive history and global recognition. First minted in 1817 and still produced today, the Sovereign was a key coin in international trade during the 19th and early 20th centuries. Its depiction of St. George slaying the dragon, designed by Benedetto Pistrucci, has become iconic, symbolizing bravery and resilience. The longevity and continuity of its production make it a linchpin in collections around the world, favored for both its numismatic and historical significance.

Each of these coins tells a unique story, a fragment of the larger human narrative captured in metal and inscriptions. They are more than currency—they are artifacts of time and tradition, shaped by the hands of artists and the currents of history, each bearing witness to the evolving saga of human civilization. As we delve further into the stories of these remarkable coins, we uncover the layers of human achievement and aspiration that are imbued in these small, metallic discs.

Coins That Changed History

Throughout history, certain coins have emerged as pivotal elements in shaping economies and influencing trade routes. For instance, consider the Spanish Real de a Ocho, also known as the "Spanish dollar" or "piece of eight." This coin, minted in the vast silver mines of the Spanish Americas during the 16th to 19th centuries, became the first global currency. Its wide circulation helped standardize exchange rates across continents, facilitating trade between Europe, the Americas, and Asia. The reliability and silver content of the Spanish dollar was so renowned that it became a benchmark monetary unit in the U.S. until the Coinage Act of 1857, which discontinued foreign coinage as legal tender. The economic influence of the Spanish dollar was profound, linking commodities markets across the world and smoothing transactions in the burgeoning global trade environment.

Another transformative coin in terms of economic impact was the British Gold Sovereign. First issued in 1817, it became a cornerstone of international finance during the 19th and early 20th centuries, particularly in the expansive British Empire. The Sovereign's high gold content and trusted minting quality made it a preferred coin for large transactions and reserves, influencing monetary systems wherever it circulated. Its role was so central to global trade that it effectively underpinned the gold standard, a monetary system in which many countries pegged the value of their currencies to a specific amount of gold, primarily held in Sovereigns. The circulation of the Gold Sovereign not only facilitated trade across the British territories but also instilled a uniform method of valuation that bolstered economic stability and growth in regions interconnected by trade.

Symbolic Coins

Coins often transcend their economic utility to embody deeper symbolic or cultural meanings. The U.S. Buffalo Nickel, minted from 1913 to 1938, serves as a poignant example. Featuring a Native American on one side and a buffalo on the other, the coin was part of an early 20th-century policy aimed at celebrating American history and culture. However, it also became a symbol of the era's contradictions—honoring the very cultures that had been marginalized by U.S. expansionist policies. Today, the Buffalo Nickel is not only a collector's item but also a token of broader socio-political discussions about heritage and representation in American numismatics.

In a similar vein, the South African Krugerrand gold coin, introduced in 1967, became symbolic of the country's complex history during apartheid. The coin, which features the face of Boer leader Paul Kruger and the Springbok antelope, was the first gold bullion coin to be minted for investment purposes, making private gold ownership accessible to the general public. However, during the 1970s and 1980s, its import was banned by many Western nations as part of economic sanctions against the apartheid regime. The Krugerrand thus embodies a dual legacy—its role in popularizing gold investment and its entanglement in the geopolitical strife of its time.

Turning Points

Coins have often been at the heart of numismatic and economic turning points. The introduction of the Euro coins in 2002, for instance, marked a significant transformation in the European economic landscape. Replacing the old currencies of twelve countries, the Euro coins were a physical manifestation of a new era in European unity and economic strategy. Their circulation was not just a monetary change but a cultural and political shift towards a more integrated Europe. The design of the coins, which includes a common side that displays the denomination and a national side that reflects the individual member state, encapsulates the tension and harmony between national identities and collective European ethos.

Another turning point came with the advent of the Canadian Loonie in 1987, named after the loon depicted on its reverse. The introduction of the one-dollar coin was part of Canada's plan to phase out paper dollars and reduce printing costs. The coin's distinctive 11-sided shape and the use of aureate-bronze plating set a new standard in coin design, combining aesthetic appeal with practical considerations like durability and cost-efficiency. The Loonie's introduction marked a significant shift in Canadian monetary practices and paved the way for the later introduction of the two-dollar coin, the Toonie.

INNOVATIVE AND PIONEERING COINS

The realm of coinage is rife with innovations that have ushered in new epochs in minting technology and design. A notable example is the Australian Polymer coins, introduced in 1988 for the country's bicentenary. These coins were the first in the world to be made from a polymer substrate, a material chosen for its durability and resistance to counterfeiting. The decision to use polymer was driven by the need to produce a coin that could withstand the harsh climatic conditions of Australia, showcasing how technological innovation in coinage often responds to environmental and economic needs.

Another groundbreaking innovation was seen in the Royal Mint's introduction of the 12-sided British one-pound coin in 2017. This coin features a complex design that includes a hologram-like image that changes from a '£' symbol to the number '1' when viewed from different angles, a feature that significantly enhances its security against counterfeits. The coin's distinctive dodecagonal shape makes it easily distinguishable by touch, an important consideration in making currency accessible to the visually impaired.

Each of these coins not only represents a leap in technological prowess but also exemplifies how the field of numismatics continuously evolves, embracing new technologies and materials to meet the changing needs of economies and societies. As collectors and enthusiasts, these coins remind us that our hobby is not just about preserving the past but also about appreciating the ingenuity and narrative of minting that continues to unfold in our times.

Numismatics: More Than Just Collecting

Numismatics, the study of coins, paper money, tokens, and medals, is a discipline that reaches far beyond the simple act of collecting. At its core, numismatics offers a unique lens through which we can explore the socio-economic, political, and cultural currents that have shaped human history. Coins, for instance, are not merely pieces of metal used for commerce; they are artifacts that carry the marks of the times they were minted, offering clues about the economic conditions, technological advancements, and artistic trends of their eras.

For you, as a collector, understanding numismatics means engaging with every coin as a chapter in the broader narrative of human civilization. Each coin you encounter tells a story, whether it's about the rise of empires, the flourishing of trade networks, or the shifts in power that have altered the course of history. This deep engagement with numismatics not only enriches your collection but also deepens your appreciation of how intricately our history is interwoven with our economies.

NUMISMATICS AND ARCHAEOLOGY

The relationship between numismatics and archaeology is particularly fascinating. Often, coins are among the most telling artifacts unearthed at archaeological sites, serving as crucial dating tools and offering insights into the trade relationships and cultural exchanges of past civilizations. For example, the discovery of Roman coins in remote parts of India has shed light on the extensive trade networks that existed between the Roman Empire and the Indian subcontinent. Similarly, coins found in Viking hoards across Northern Europe not only speak to the Vikings' raiding and trading but also to their connections with the Islamic world, as evidenced by the Arabic inscriptions on many of the coins. For historians and archaeologists, these findings are invaluable, as they provide concrete, datable evidence of historical interactions that might not be documented elsewhere. As a collector, when you come across coins that might have been buried for centuries, you're essentially touching a piece of history that has been part of human stories across time and space, possibly influencing or reflecting significant historical events.

Preserving Heritage

Numismatics also plays a critical role in the preservation of cultural heritage. Each coin is a preservation of the art, craftsmanship, and aesthetic preferences of the period in which it was created. Collecting coins is thus not merely a hobby but a form of guardianship over these small yet significant ambassadors of our past. By maintaining and curating a coin collection, you are helping to preserve these artifacts for future generations, ensuring that the cultural and historical knowledge they carry is not lost. This aspect of numismatics is what often inspires museums and educational institutions to invest in numismatic collections. These collections serve as tangible connections to our past, providing educational material that can help people understand and appreciate the depth and diversity of human history.

Academic and Research Opportunities

The field of numismatics is not just about collecting but also contributes significantly to academic research. Many numismatists are scholars and historians who use coins as primary source materials for their research on various aspects of history. As a collector, you have the opportunity to contribute to this body of knowledge. This could be through the discovery of a rare coin that sheds new light on a particular historical period or through the detailed study of a series of coins that offer insights into the economic fluctuations of a forgotten kingdom. Furthermore, the academic community often values the detailed cataloging and preservation efforts of serious collectors, as these collections can provide valuable data for research studies. Collaborations between academic institutions and collectors can lead to exciting discoveries and enrich the field of numismatics with shared knowledge and resources. Engaging in such research not only enhances the academic value of your collection but also contributes to a deeper understanding of history shared by scholars and enthusiasts alike.

As we wrap up this exploration into the rich world of numismatics, remember that each coin in your collection does more than just add value; it carries a piece of history, an artifact of human civilization that has witnessed the ebb and flow of cultures, economies, and empires. By engaging with numismatics, you are not only indulging in a hobby but are also preserving and studying the legacies left behind by our ancestors. This chapter hopefully has broadened your perspective on what it means to be a collector and the significant role you play in the continuum of history.

In the next chapter, we will delve into the practical aspects of preserving your coin collection, ensuring that each piece remains as impeccable as the day it was minted or discovered. This journey into preservation is not just about maintaining value; it's about respecting the history and artistry that each coin represents, securing a legacy that can be cherished for generations to come.

CHAPTER SIX

PRESERVING YOUR COLLECTION

In the intricate world of coin collecting, each coin not only represents a piece of history but also an investment of both time and resources. The thrill of acquiring a new piece for your collection is unmatched, yet the true challenge—and indeed, the skill—lies in maintaining the pristine condition of these treasures. Preserving your collection is akin to safeguarding a delicate legacy; it's about more than just avoiding physical damage. It's about ensuring that each coin continues to tell its story for generations to come. In this chapter, we will delve into the fundamental aspects of coin handling and care, equipping you with the knowledge to protect your collection from common hazards and unforeseen accidents.

BASIC COIN HANDLING AND CARE

Handling your coins correctly is critical to preserving their condition and value. Every time a coin is touched, there's a risk of transferring oils and acids from your skin onto the metal, which can cause corrosion over time. To minimize direct contact, always hold coins by their edges, using your thumb and forefinger. This technique reduces the exposure of the coin's faces to direct skin contact, thereby protecting its surfaces from fingerprints and smudges, which are not just unsightly but potentially damaging.

It's also prudent to wear gloves when handling coins, particularly those made of cotton or special lint-free, acid-free gloves designed for handling numismatic materials. These gloves provide an additional layer of protection, preventing oils from your skin from contacting the coin while also reducing the risk of dropping them due to slippery fingers. Whenever you handle coins, ensure that you do so over a padded surface. This simple precaution can prevent a minor slip from becoming a catastrophic fall, potentially denting or scratching your valuable coins.

Cleaning Dos and Don'ts

One of the most common mistakes new collectors make is improperly cleaning their coins. While it might seem intuitive to clean a dirty or tarnished coin, improper cleaning can actually do more harm than good. Abrasive cleaning methods, such as scrubbing with a brush or using harsh chemicals, can leave scratches or cause pitting, significantly diminishing a coin's aesthetic and market value.

If you believe a coin needs cleaning, first assess whether it's necessary. Often, what might appear as dirt or tarnish to the untrained eye could actually be a natural patina that develops over time, which can add to the coin's character and authenticity. If cleaning is absolutely necessary, consult a professional or use only mild soaps and warm water, and handle the coin as little as possible during the cleaning process. Pat the coin dry with a soft, lint-free cloth instead of rubbing it to avoid scratches.

Regular Maintenance

Regular maintenance is essential to keep your collection in top condition. Schedule periodic reviews of your collection to inspect each coin for signs of wear, environmental damage, or other issues. Use a magnifying glass to examine your coins closely, looking for any signs of deterioration that might not be visible to the naked eye.

During these inspections, it's also a good time to update your collection inventory. Keeping a detailed record of each coin, including its condition, storage location, and any other pertinent details, can help you manage your collection more effectively. This documentation can be invaluable for insurance purposes, future sales, or even just for personal tracking of your collection's growth and evolution.

Emergency Care

Accidents happen, and knowing how to respond when a coin is exposed to potentially damaging substances can save you a lot of distress and expense. If a coin comes into contact with harmful chemicals, immediately rinse it with distilled water. Avoid tap water if possible, as it may contain minerals or chemicals that could cause further damage. After rinsing, air dry the coin on a soft, lint-free cloth.

In cases where a coin is dropped or physically altered, resist the urge to correct any bends or dents yourself. Amateur attempts at repairing physical damage can exacerbate the issue. Instead, consult a professional conservator who specializes in numismatic items. These experts can provide advice or services to restore the coin's condition without inflicting further damage.

Maintaining the integrity of your coin collection is a continuous commitment that requires careful handling, regular maintenance, and the foresight to address problems before they escalate. By adopting these practices, you not only preserve the physical condition of your coins but also protect their historical significance and monetary value. This thoughtful approach to preservation ensures that your collection can continue to provide joy and value for many years to come, becoming a legacy of your passion for numismatics.

STORAGE SOLUTIONS FOR EVERY COLLECTOR

As a coin collector, you understand that the way you store your coins is just as crucial as how you handle them. Different storage methods cater to varying needs, from ensuring long-term preservation to showcasing your collection's beauty. Let's explore the array of storage options available, weighing their benefits and drawbacks to help you make informed decisions tailored to your collection's specific requirements.

Starting with the simplest storage method, coin flips are inexpensive and widely used among collectors. These are small, plastic pouches that allow you to view the coin without removing it from its protective covering. While flips are cost-effective and great for less valuable coins, they are not always acid-free, which can be a concern. Some plastics used in cheaper flips might release harmful chemicals over time, potentially damaging your coins. Therefore, it's advisable to opt for flips made from Mylar or other inert materials that provide safer long-term storage.

For those with a more significant investment in their collection, high-end cases offer robust protection and an aesthetically pleasing display option. These cases are typically crafted from high-quality materials with interiors lined with soft, acid-free fabrics to prevent any scratching or chemical damage to the coins. The major downside is the cost, as these cases can be quite an investment in themselves. However, for valuable, rare, or sentimental pieces, the expense can be justified by the superior protection and elegant presentation they offer.

Another sophisticated option is slabbed coins, which are sealed within protective, tamper-proof plastic by professional grading services. This method is highly regarded for its ability to preserve the coin's condition and authenticate its grade. While slabbing is more expensive, it's a prudent choice for particularly valuable or delicate coins, as it virtually eliminates the risk of physical or chemical damage.

Now, moving onto the critical aspect of climate control in coin storage. Maintaining the right temperature and humidity levels is paramount to preserving the integrity of your coin collection. Coins are susceptible to damage from extreme temperatures and fluctuations in humidity, which can accelerate deterioration and promote harmful chemical reactions. Ideally, your coins should be stored in a cool, dry place where the temperature and humidity levels are stable. A controlled environment can be achieved using air-tight containers with silica gel packs to absorb any excess moisture or more sophisticated climate-controlled safes or storage rooms designed specifically for collectibles. Implementing these measures can significantly extend the lifespan of your collection, ensuring that each piece remains in pristine condition.

Organizing and cataloging your collection effectively is another pivotal aspect of coin storage. Proper organization not only facilitates easier access and tracking of your coins but also enhances the enjoyment of your collecting experience. Consider categorizing your coins by date, region, or type and using labeled dividers in your storage cases or drawers. Implementing a digital or physical cataloging system where you log each coin's details, such as condition, purchase date, price, and provenance, can be incredibly beneficial. This organized approach not only helps in managing your collection efficiently but also prepares you for potential future appraisals, sales, or exhibitions.

For those who prefer to display their coins, choosing the right setup is crucial to balance aesthetics with preservation. Display cases with UV-protective glass can prevent sunlight damage while positioning your displays away from direct sunlight and high-traffic areas can minimize the risk of environmental damage or accidental knocks. It's important to use mounts or stands that do not exert pressure on the coins, opting instead for custom holders that provide support without stress. While displaying your collection can be immensely satisfying, ensuring that these precautions are in place is essential to avoid compromising the coins' condition.

Choosing the right storage solutions requires a blend of practicality, budget consideration, and foresight. Whether you opt for simple flips for everyday coins or invest in high-end cases for treasures, the key is to tailor your choices to the specific needs of your collection. By implementing effective climate control measures and organizing your coins thoughtfully, you not only safeguard their physical and aesthetic qualities but also enhance the overall value and enjoyment of your numismatic journey. Remember, each coin in your collection is a piece of history and art; preserving them with care allows you to cherish and share this legacy indefinitely.

ENVIRONMENTAL CONSIDERATIONS

Understanding the myriad environmental risks that can impact the integrity of your coin collection is critical for any collector. Factors such as moisture, sunlight, and environmental pollutants can degrade coins over time, sometimes irreversibly. Moisture, for instance, is particularly nefarious for coin collections as it can lead to corrosion and tarnish, especially for coins made from copper and silver. This kind of damage not only diminishes the aesthetic appeal of the coins but can also significantly reduce their market value. Sunlight, or more specifically the ultraviolet light it contains, can cause fading and deterioration of the delicate surfaces of coins, while pollutants like smoke or chemical vapors can create a layer of grime that etches into the metal over time or cause harmful reactions that compromise the coin's surface.

To safeguard your collection from these risks, several protective measures can be implemented. The use of dehumidifiers in areas where your coins are stored can help control the ambient humidity levels, reducing the risk of moisture-related damage. For collectors living in particularly humid climates, small silica gel packets can also be placed inside coin storage containers to absorb excess moisture. Protecting coins from sunlight is equally important. Storing your collection in a dark, cool place away from direct sunlight prevents the harmful effects of UV exposure. For added protection, especially if your coins are displayed, consider using UV-protective cases or glass for display cabinets. These materials can significantly block or absorb ultraviolet light, offering an extra layer of defense against light exposure.

In terms of air quality, ensure that your storage environment is free from pollutants. This can mean storing your collection in an area away from kitchen fumes, smoke, or chemical vapors, which are common in garages or basements where other items might be emitting harmful substances. Air purifiers can be an excellent investment in such scenarios, helping to maintain a clean and stable environment around your coins. Furthermore, for highly valuable or especially delicate coins, inert gas storage solutions, such as nitrogen or argon cabinets, can provide an atmosphere free of any reactive gases, virtually eliminating the risk of environmental degradation.

Creating the ideal environment for storing your coins involves more than just addressing immediate threats; it also requires a proactive approach to maintenance. Regularly monitoring the storage conditions of your collection is essential. This can be as simple as keeping a hygrometer in the storage area to check humidity levels or using a UV light meter to assess the exposure levels in display areas. Digital tools and smart home devices offer automated monitoring solutions where environmental conditions can be tracked and adjusted remotely, ensuring optimal conditions are maintained consistently.

Adjustments to your storage setup might be necessary as your collection grows or as environmental conditions change. For instance, shifting seasons might influence indoor humidity or temperature, necessitating a reassessment of your current protective measures. Being vigilant and responsive to these changes is crucial. Regular checks and maintenance not only keep your collection in pristine condition but also imbibe a discipline that is fundamental to successful coin collecting. By understanding and managing the environmental factors that can affect your coins, you ensure that your collection not only maintains its historical and aesthetic value but is also preserved for future generations to appreciate and enjoy.

INSURANCE AND DOCUMENTATION

Accumulating a coin collection is a source of pride and joy, reflecting not only a significant monetary investment but also an emotional attachment to each piece's unique story and heritage. As your collection grows, so does the importance of properly documenting and insuring it. This not only protects your financial investment but also ensures that the legacy and scholarly value of your collection are preserved.

Documenting your collection thoroughly is essential for multiple reasons. Firstly, it aids in managing your collection effectively, allowing you to keep track of what you own, its condition, and its provenance. This is particularly valuable for insurance purposes, where detailed records and proof of ownership are necessary. Secondly, for legacy purposes, a well-documented collection can be a significant asset, making the process of bequeathing or selling parts of your collection much smoother. Lastly, from a scholarly perspective, detailed documentation contributes to the numismatic community by providing data and research material that can be used in academic studies and publications.

To start documenting your collection, maintain a detailed ledger or use a digital inventory system that includes high-quality photographs of each coin, purchase details, current condition reports, and any historical information you have. This record should be updated regularly as new pieces are added or as existing pieces are sold or change condition. For added security, store copies of your documentation in different locations, such as in a safe deposit box and digitally in the cloud, to ensure that the information is preserved in case of physical damage to one set of records.

Valuing your collection accurately is another critical aspect of coin collecting. Regular appraisals by certified professionals can provide up-to-date values that reflect the current market conditions, which can fluctuate significantly over time. These appraisals are crucial for insurance purposes, ensuring that your policy covers the full value of your collection. It's advisable to seek appraisals from reputable sources within the numismatic community who understand the nuances of rare and antique coins. Additionally, attending coin shows and staying active in numismatic circles can provide insights into current trends and values, helping you to keep your appraisals current.

Choosing the right insurance for your collection is vital. Standard homeowner's insurance policies often do not cover collectibles adequately, or they may have limits that are too low for valuable collections. Specialized collectibles insurance is available and can be tailored to the specific needs of coin collectors. These policies typically offer more comprehensive coverage, including against risks such as accidental damage, theft, and even natural disasters, which might not be covered under standard policies. When selecting an insurance provider, compare different policies to see what is covered and what exclusions apply. Check the provider's reputation within the industry and their process for handling claims, particularly for collectibles, to ensure that they have the expertise to deal with potential issues specific to numismatic collections.

Legal considerations also play a significant role in managing your collection, especially concerning inheritance and tax implications. Consulting with a legal advisor who specializes in estate planning and collectibles is prudent. They can help you understand the legal framework surrounding your collection, advise on structuring ownership to optimize tax implications and assist in setting up a will or trust that includes your collection. This is particularly important if you wish your collection to be kept intact or donated to a museum or academic institution.

By taking these steps to document, value, insure, and legally protect your collection, you ensure not only its physical safety but also its lasting value and contribution to the numismatic community. This proactive approach allows you to enjoy your collection with the peace of mind that comes from knowing it is well-cared for and that its legacy is secure.

As we conclude this chapter on preserving your collection, we reaffirm the importance of a meticulous approach to handling, storing, documenting, and insuring your treasured coins. Each step you take in this direction not only safeguards your investment but also enriches your experience as a collector. The upcoming chapter will delve into the exciting world of coin trading and selling, where you will learn how to navigate the market dynamics to optimize your collection's potential. This next step in your numismatic journey promises to be as rewarding as it is enlightening, offering new opportunities for growth and discovery in the vast world of coin collecting.

UNLOCK THE POWER OF GENEROSITY

"Sharing knowledge is the most fundamental act of friendship. Because it is a way you can give something without losing something." - Richard Stallman

People who give without expecting anything in return lead happier, more fulfilling lives. So, let's take a moment to spread some kindness. Would you help someone you've never met, even if you never got credit for it? Who is this person? They might be a lot like you were once—new to coin collecting, eager to learn, but not sure where to start. Our mission is to make coin collecting accessible and enjoyable for everyone. To achieve this, we need to reach as many people as possible.

This is where you come in. Most people judge a book by its cover and its reviews. So here's a small request on behalf of a budding coin collector you've never met:

Please help that new collector by leaving this book a review.

Your review won't cost you anything and will take less than 60 seconds, but it can make a huge difference. Your words could help...

- One more child discover the joy of history through coins.

- One more parent bond with their child over a shared hobby.

- One more enthusiast gain the confidence to start their collection.

- One more student ace their school project on numismatics.

- One more collector turn their passion into a rewarding investment.

To feel that 'feel good' moment and really help someone, all you have to do is leave a review. It takes less than 60 seconds.

Simply scan the QR code below to leave your review:

or click here on your devices

If helping a fellow coin enthusiast makes you feel good, you're our kind of person. Welcome to the club. You're one of us.

I'm excited to help you explore the fascinating world of coin collecting faster and easier than you can imagine. You'll love the tips and stories shared in the coming chapters.

Thank you from the bottom of my heart. Now, back to our journey into the world of coins.

- Your biggest fan, David Green

PS - Fun fact: If you provide something of value to another person, it makes you more valuable to them. If you'd like goodwill straight from another coin collector - and you believe this book will help them - send this book their way.

CHAPTER SEVEN

THE COIN-COLLECTING COMMUNITY

In the vibrant world of coin collecting, the shared enthusiasm and knowledge within collector communities often become the heartbeat of the hobby. Whether you're a seasoned numismatist or a newcomer eager to dive deeper, the collective wisdom of coin clubs and societies can significantly enrich your collecting experience. These organizations act not just as gathering points but as invaluable reservoirs of knowledge, camaraderie, and support. By engaging with these communities, you open doors to a myriad of opportunities and experiences that go beyond the solitary act of collecting.

JOINING COIN CLUBS AND SOCIETIES

Choosing the right coin club or society to join can significantly impact your collecting journey. Start by identifying what you hope to gain from membership. Are you looking for educational opportunities or perhaps a focus on a specific type of coin or period in history? You may be seeking a community with whom you can share and grow your collection. Once you have a clear idea of your objectives, research local and national organizations that align with your interests. Local libraries, coin shops, and even online platforms can provide information on nearby clubs. Many national or international societies also have local chapters, which can be a perfect blend of broad resources and local community.

When evaluating different clubs, consider attending a few meetings as a guest. This can give you a feel for the club's culture, the expertise of its members, and the type of activities they offer. Look for clubs that provide a structured yet welcoming environment with a mix of educational programs, discussions, auctions, and social events. These activities not only enhance your knowledge and collection but also make your membership a rewarding and enjoyable experience.

Benefits of Membership

Joining a coin club or society comes with a plethora of benefits. Educationally, these organizations often host lectures, workshops, and presentations by seasoned collectors and professionals in the numismatics field. These sessions can provide deeper insights into aspects of collecting that are not easily accessible through books or online research, such as grading nuances, market trends, and historical contexts.

Access to resources is another significant benefit. Many clubs have libraries with specialized books, magazines, and newsletters that are otherwise expensive or difficult to obtain. Additionally, membership often provides opportunities to participate in exclusive auctions and access to dealer networks that can help you acquire rare pieces at fair prices.

Community is perhaps the most enriching benefit. Coin collecting can be a solitary activity, but through clubs, you connect with like-minded individuals who share your passion. These relationships can lead to mentorships, friendships, and invaluable networking opportunities that can assist you in your collecting endeavors. The shared experiences and stories add a rich layer of enjoyment to your hobby.

Contributing to the Community

Active participation in a coin club or society not only enhances your own experience but also contributes to the vitality of the community. Consider volunteering for positions within the club, such as event coordination or newsletter editing. Sharing your knowledge through presentations or informal discussions can also be incredibly valuable to fellow members. Engaging actively in club activities not only helps the organization thrive but also deepens your own connection to the hobby, enriching your experience and opening up new avenues in your collecting journey.

LOCAL VS. NATIONAL ORGANIZATIONS

The choice between joining a local club or a national organization can depend on your specific needs and goals. Local clubs offer the advantage of regular face-to-face interactions and the ability to form close-knit relationships with collectors in your area. These clubs often focus on community building and may have more frequent meetings, making it easier to stay continually engaged.

National or international societies, on the other hand, typically provide broader resources, including larger conventions, more extensive libraries, and connections to a wider network of collectors. These organizations can offer a more structured approach to education and certification programs that might be beneficial for those looking to take a more professional or investment-oriented approach to collecting.

In many cases, a combination of both types of memberships can be beneficial. Local clubs provide community and regular engagement, while national societies offer depth and extensive resources. By navigating these community networks, you enhance not just your collection but also your overall enjoyment and understanding of the numismatic world. This rich tapestry of interactions and learning is what makes coin collecting a uniquely rewarding hobby.

Coin Shows

Attending your first coin show can be as exhilarating as it is overwhelming. Picture a bustling hall filled with displays of gleaming coins, each piece holding stories of eras gone by. For many collectors, coin shows are the highlight of their numismatic activities, offering a treasure trove of opportunities to view, buy, and learn about diverse coins from various dealers and fellow enthusiasts. Typically, these events range from small local gatherings to large international expos featuring a wide array of coins, paper money, and numismatic literature. As a newcomer, expect a sensory-rich environment where history and commerce blend seamlessly. You'll encounter a variety of sellers and buyers, from casual hobbyists to serious investors and professional dealers, all united by a passion for collecting.

Navigating a coin show effectively begins long before you step into the venue. Preparation is key. Start by researching the event details—know the date, location, and schedule of the show. Many shows offer special sessions, such as educational talks or workshops, which can greatly enhance your experience. It's wise to set a budget before you go. With the myriad of tempting offers, it's easy to get swept away. Having a clear idea of what you're willing to spend helps in making thoughtful, informed decisions. When you arrive, take a moment to get your bearings. Pick up a map of the dealer booths, and perhaps plan a route that allows you to see everything you're interested in without backtracking. Take your time to browse through the coins; this is a perfect chance to see a wide variety in person, which can be invaluable for a beginner.

While the array of choices can be exciting, the art of negotiation is also a critical aspect of the coin show experience. Prices at shows often have a little flexibility built in. It's acceptable and expected to politely negotiate on items that catch your interest. Start by asking if the price listed is the best they can offer. Often, dealers are willing to lower the price slightly to secure a sale, especially towards the end of the show. However, it's crucial to remain respectful and reasonable—offering an absurdly low price can be seen as insulting and may shut down negotiations. If you're serious about a piece but still unsure, don't hesitate to ask questions about its history, condition, or value. Most dealers are passionate about coins and enjoy sharing their knowledge. Moreover, they can provide insights that might not be evident from just looking at the coin.

Coin shows are also governed by an unspoken code of conduct to ensure that transactions and interactions go smoothly. Etiquette at these events is mostly common sense but important to adhere to for a positive experience. Always ask for permission before handling someone else's coins, and handle them carefully—preferably with gloves. Be mindful of others' space and privacy when at a booth or table, keeping in mind that everyone is there to enjoy the show. If you bring children, keep an eye on them to ensure they don't accidentally damage any items. Remember, a polite and friendly attitude goes a long way in making connections and learning from others.

Speaking of learning, coin shows are ripe with opportunities for networking. They are a gathering of experts and enthusiasts, each with their own experiences and specialties. Engaging in conversations can lead to new friendships, mentorships, and even future trading partners. Don't be shy about introducing yourself and sharing your interests. More experienced collectors often appreciate the enthusiasm of newcomers and can provide advice that could steer your collecting journey toward more fruitful directions. Collect business cards, join discussions, and if you feel inclined, share your own experiences and knowledge. Networking at these shows can significantly broaden your understanding of numismatics and open doors to new opportunities within the collecting community.

By approaching your first coin show with a prepared, respectful, and open-minded attitude, you stand to gain not just interesting additions to your collection but valuable knowledge and connections that could enhance your collecting journey in ways you never anticipated. As you move from booth to booth, absorbing the rich tapestry of stories and transactions, remember that each interaction, each coin, adds a layer of depth to your understanding of this fascinating hobby.

ONLINE FORUMS AND SOCIAL NETWORKS

In the digital age, the landscape of coin collecting has expanded beyond physical meetings and shows to vibrant online communities. These platforms offer a dynamic space where collectors can share, learn, and connect with others globally. Understanding how to navigate and leverage these online forums and social networks can significantly enhance your collecting experience, providing access to a wealth of information and a broader network of like-minded enthusiasts.

The first step in leveraging online communities is choosing the right platforms. Numerous forums are dedicated to numismatics, each with its own focus and community vibe. For example, the Coin Community Forum is known for its friendly atmosphere and wide range of topics, making it ideal for both beginners and seasoned collectors. Another notable platform is the Collectors Universe Forum, which attracts more advanced collectors with a focus on grading and authentication discussions. When selecting a forum, consider what matches your interests and level of expertise. Spend some time browsing the discussions to get a feel for the community's tone and the type of content that's shared.

Once you've found forums that resonate with your collecting goals, it's crucial to understand how to engage effectively. Start by introducing yourself in the designated introduction threads. Share a bit about your interests and what you hope to gain from the community. When you begin participating in discussions, always strive to bring value. Whether it's by sharing your own knowledge, asking insightful questions, or providing helpful links and resources, the goal is to contribute positively to the community. Remember, the more you engage, the more you benefit, as active participation often leads to deeper insights and stronger connections.

Navigating online communities also requires an awareness of safety, particularly regarding privacy and scams. Protect your personal information by using a pseudonym or handle instead of your real name, and be cautious about sharing details that could lead to identity theft or fraud. Be especially vigilant when discussions involve buying or selling coins. Verify the credibility of sellers or buyers through their post history and feedback from other community members. Many forums have feedback systems in place or designated threads where members can report successful trades, which can be a valuable resource for verifying trustworthiness.

Furthermore, the risk of scams is not negligible. Be wary of deals that seem too good to be true, such as rare coins being sold significantly under market value. Always use secure payment methods that offer buyer protection, and consider using an escrow service for higher-value transactions. By staying informed and cautious, you can enjoy the benefits of online communities while minimizing the risks.

As you become more comfortable and established within these online spaces, consider exploring additional features many forums offer, such as virtual meetups, webinars, and live auctions. These events can be fantastic opportunities to deepen your knowledge and connections within the community. Engaging regularly and meaningfully in these online forums not only enhances your own collecting experience but also contributes to the vibrancy and richness of the numismatic community at large. Through these digital interactions, you continue to build a network that supports and enriches your passion for coin collecting, bridging geographical divides and connecting you with fellow enthusiasts around the world.

Sharing Your Collection

In the age of digital connectivity, social media platforms have emerged as powerful tools for sharing your passion with a global audience. As a coin collector, these platforms offer you unique opportunities to display your collection, connect with other enthusiasts, and even learn from experts worldwide. However, navigating social media requires a strategic approach to maximize benefits while safeguarding your valuable collection.

Engaging with Social Media

The allure of sharing your coin collection on social media lies in its ability to reach a vast audience effortlessly. Platforms like Instagram, Facebook, and Twitter are not only venues for exhibition but also spaces where you can attract feedback, initiate discussions, and participate in global numismatic communities. Sharing your collection can help you gain recognition as a collector and can open doors to new learning and trading opportunities.

However, social media has its pitfalls. The visibility of sharing online can attract not only fellow enthusiasts but also potential fraudsters. Thus, it's crucial to balance openness with caution. Engage your audience with interesting content about your collection without revealing sensitive information, such as high-resolution images of extremely rare or valuable coins, which could be used for counterfeiting purposes. Keep personal details such as your location, purchasing habits, or storage practices private to avoid risks of theft or targeted scams.

Photography Tips

Effective social media engagement heavily relies on visual appeal, especially on platforms like Instagram or Pinterest, where imagery is paramount. Here are some tips to help you showcase your coins in the best light:

1- Lighting: Good lighting is critical for highlighting the intricate details of coins. Natural light often provides the best results, but avoid direct sunlight as it can cause harsh shadows. A soft, diffused light can accentuate the relief and luster of coins without creating glare.

2- Background: Use a neutral background that doesn't distract from the coin itself. Simple solid colors like black, white, or grey are choices that enhance the coin's features without competing for attention.

3- Focus and Clarity: Ensure your camera or smartphone is focused precisely on the coin. Blurry or out-of-focus photos can detract from the details that make your coins unique. If your device has a macro lens feature, use it to capture the fine details.

4- Angles: Experiment with different angles to capture the depth and texture of coins. Sometimes, a slight tilt or an angled shot can reveal aspects of a coin that a straight-on view cannot.

By mastering the art of coin photography, you not only enhance the aesthetic appeal of your posts but also provide your audience with a richer visual experience that can foster engagement and appreciation.

Building a Following

Growing a following on social media involves more than just posting beautiful images of your coins; it requires building relationships and consistently engaging with your audience. Share stories behind your coins—why you chose them, their historical significance, or any personal anecdotes related to them. These narratives add depth to your posts and make your collection more relatable and interesting.

Regularly engage with your followers by responding to comments, asking questions, and participating in relevant discussions. This interaction helps build a community around your collection, fostering loyalty and increasing engagement. Additionally, use relevant hashtags or participate in popular coin-collecting challenges or themes to reach a broader audience interested in numismatics.

Taking Precautions

While social media opens up new avenues for sharing and learning, it also necessitates precautions to protect your collection. Be selective about what you post. Avoid sharing overly detailed images or information about the most valuable or rare items in your collection that could attract the wrong kind of attention. Consider watermarking your images to prevent misuse and to establish ownership.

Furthermore, be cautious about sharing personal information or specifics about your transactions and trades. Keep details of your buying or selling activities private and conduct negotiations or transactions through private messages or, better yet, through secure trading platforms.

Social media, when used wisely, can be a fantastic tool for sharing your passion for coin collecting and connecting with a community that shares your interests. By taking thoughtful steps to present your collection attractively and safely, you can enjoy the wide-reaching benefits of these platforms while minimizing potential risks.

As this chapter closes, remember that each post you share not only showcases your collection but also contributes to the rich tapestry of the global numismatic community. Looking ahead, the next chapter will delve into understanding the coin market, providing you with insights and strategies to navigate buying, selling, and trading in the dynamic world of coin collecting. This knowledge will equip you to make informed decisions, enhancing both your collection and your enjoyment of this fascinating hobby.

CHAPTER EIGHT

UNDERSTANDING THE COIN MARKET

Navigating the coin market can feel akin to sailing a vast ocean: the currents of supply and demand constantly shift, and understanding these dynamics is crucial for any collector aiming to capitalize on their investments. As you delve deeper into the world of numismatics, gaining an insight into the economic forces at play can transform your collecting from a passive hobby to an active, informed pursuit. This journey into the market mechanics of coin collecting will equip you with the knowledge needed to recognize value, anticipate market trends, and make strategic decisions that align with both your passion and investment goals.

The Economics of Coin Collecting

The fundamental economic principle of supply and demand is vividly at play in the coin market. Essentially, the value of a coin is heavily influenced by its rarity (supply) and the number of collectors eager to acquire it (demand). For instance, a coin that was minted in limited quantities or a series that was prematurely discontinued will often have a higher value due to its scarce availability. Conversely, a coin that exists in large quantities may only fetch a high price if it becomes highly sought after for reasons such as historical significance or unique features.

The interplay between supply and demand can lead to significant fluctuations in coin prices. For instance, when a new hoard of previously rare coins is discovered, the increased supply can cause prices to drop. Similarly, a surge in popularity of a certain era or type of coin can lead to increased demand, driving up prices. This was seen when the 50 State Quarters program released by the U.S. Mint sparked renewed interest in quarter collecting, significantly increasing the market value of certain quarters.

Rarity and Desirability

Rarity alone does not dictate a coin's value; desirability plays an equally crucial role. A coin might be rare because few were minted, but if there is little collector interest, its market value may remain low. Conversely, some coins may be relatively common but highly desired due to factors such as their historical context, aesthetic appeal, or role in popular collecting themes, which can elevate their market value significantly.

Take, for example, the 1943 copper penny. While the majority of pennies minted that year were made of steel due to wartime metal rationing, a few were mistakenly struck in copper, making them extremely rare. Their desirability, coupled with their fascinating error-based backstory, makes them highly sought after and valuable among collectors. This highlights how rarity and desirability are intertwined, each influencing a coin's appeal and, consequently, its market value.

Market Fluctuations

The coin market is not isolated from the broader economic landscape and can be influenced by various external factors. Economic downturns, for example, can lead collectors to sell off parts of their collections, increasing supply and potentially lowering market values. Conversely, during economic booms, more individuals may have disposable income to spend on hobbies like coin collecting, driving up demand and prices.

Collector trends also significantly impact market dynamics. The emergence of new collecting trends can suddenly increase demand for certain types of coins. For instance, the rise in popularity of ancient Roman coins can be attributed to more widespread interest in ancient cultures fuelled by movies, books, and educational content. Staying attuned to these trends is crucial for collectors looking to acquire new pieces and decide the optimal timing for selling parts of their collections.

IDENTIFYING MARKET OPPORTUNITIES

To capitalize on market opportunities, you must first stay informed about market conditions and trends. Regularly visiting coin shows, participating in online forums, and subscribing to numismatic publications can provide insights into what coins are in demand and what might be a good investment.

When considering a purchase, look for coins that have a consistent history of demand and are likely to appreciate in value. Coins with historical significance, aesthetic appeal, or those that are part of a popular series, often make good candidates. Additionally, consider the timing of your purchases; buying during a market dip, when prices are generally lower, can provide better returns on investment.

Selling coins also requires strategic timing. Monitor the market to determine when your coins have reached a peak in value. This might be during an anniversary related to the coin's theme or following a surge in popularity of a particular coin type. Selling during such peaks can maximize your returns.

By understanding the market dynamics of coin collecting, you can make more informed decisions, turning your passion for numismatics into a profitable venture. As you continue to navigate this complex market, remember that each coin not only represents a piece of history but also an opportunity—an opportunity to grow your collection, expand your knowledge, and perhaps enhance your financial well-being.

Staying Updated on Market Trends

Understanding the coin market requires a steadfast commitment to staying informed about the latest trends and shifts. This is not just about keeping a tab on prices; it's about understanding why those prices change and how various factors contribute to those changes. The most successful collectors use a combination of resources to keep their knowledge current and relevant. One of the primary resources is numismatic publications and websites. Magazines such as "Coin World" or "Numismatic News" offer a wealth of information, including market analyses, upcoming auction details, and reports on recent finds. Websites like the Professional Coin Grading Service (PCGS) provide databases and price guides that are updated in real time, offering you a snapshot of current market conditions.

In addition to publications, engaging with online platforms that aggregate data on coin sales across different auction houses can provide a comprehensive view of the market. These platforms often feature tools that allow you to track price trends over time, giving you insights into how certain types of coins are appreciating or depreciating. This kind of detailed tracking can be invaluable when you are deciding whether to buy or sell a particular piece. It's also useful for spotting patterns in the market, such as a surge in interest for coins from a specific era or mint, which could indicate a burgeoning trend you might want to capitalize on.

The Role of Auctions

Auctions play a critical role in the coin-collecting market, serving as both a barometer for current valuations and a forecast for future trends. By following auction results, you can glean insights into what collectors are currently valuing highly and how certain coins are performing in the open market. For example, if a particular coin consistently exceeds estimated values at auctions, it might signal increasing collector interest or a decrease in available pieces. Conversely, if coins begin to sell for less than their estimated value, it might indicate a cooling interest or an oversupply in the market.

Auction houses also often provide catalogs and post-sale reports that can be studied to understand better the factors contributing to a coin's final price. These reports can include expert insights into the coin's provenance, condition, and historical significance, which are all factors that can influence its market value. Engaging with these materials can enhance your ability to assess coins, both at auctions and in private sales, improving your strategic decision-making over time.

Networking with Experts

While publications and auctions provide a wealth of information, nothing is as valuable as the firsthand insights gained from networking with experienced dealers and fellow collectors. These individuals often have years, if not decades, of experience and can provide nuanced understandings of the market that you won't find in publications or online databases. Relationships with dealers can be particularly beneficial—they can offer you first dibs on newly acquired coins, provide background stories that add to a coin's value, and give personalized advice based on their knowledge of your collection's strengths and gaps.

Attending coin shows, joining numismatic clubs, and participating in online forums are excellent ways to meet and engage with these experts. Over time, these relationships can evolve into mentorships, offering you ongoing guidance and education that is tailored to your specific interests and goals in the world of coin collecting. Moreover, these connections can sometimes lead to opportunities for private trades or purchases, where you can acquire valuable pieces at prices more favorable than those in public markets.

Analyzing Historical Data

To truly understand market trends and make predictions about future movements, analyzing historical price data is indispensable. This involves more than just looking at price increases or decreases; it requires a deep dive into the contexts that caused these changes. For example, understanding how geopolitical events, economic downturns, or changes in consumer behavior have historically affected coin prices can help you anticipate how future events might impact your investments.

Tools like historical price charts, which plot the prices of certain coins over many years, can be particularly enlightening. They allow you to see how coins similar to those in your collection have appreciated over time, providing a blueprint for what might happen to your coins in the future. Additionally, studying auction archives can reveal long-term trends in collector interest and market saturation, helping you decide when to sell a piece or when to seek out specific coins that might be poised for appreciation.

By dedicating time to understanding these various elements of market trends—utilizing a mix of current resources, auction data, expert insights, and historical analysis—you position yourself not just as a collector but as a savvy participant in the numismatic market. This proactive approach not only enhances your enjoyment of the hobby but also maximizes the potential returns on your investments, making every decision an informed one in the ever-evolving landscape of coin collecting.

RISKS AND REWARDS OF INVESTING IN COINS

Investing in coins is a fascinating endeavor that blends the thrill of numismatic discovery with the strategic acumen of financial investment. However, like any investment, it comes with its own set of risks and rewards, which you, as an investor, must navigate wisely to achieve success. Understanding these risks and how to mitigate them is crucial in developing a resilient investment strategy. Market volatility can significantly impact the value of coins. The numismatic market is susceptible to shifts in economic conditions, collector interest, and even geopolitical events, which can all influence coin prices. For instance, an economic downturn can reduce collector spending power, leading to decreased demand and lower coin prices. Conversely, a surge in interest in certain historical periods or types of coins can drive prices up. Liquidity issues also pose a risk; unlike stocks or bonds, coins can be harder to sell quickly without potentially incurring a loss, especially if you need to liquidate your investment in a hurry.

To counterbalance these risks, diversifying your coin portfolio is a strategic move. Just as with traditional investments, diversification in numismatics can help absorb shocks in turbulent times. This involves spreading your investments across a variety of coin types, time periods, and even geographical regions. For example, while you might invest heavily in U.S. coins, considering adding ancient coins or foreign coins can offer protection against fluctuations in the U.S. market. Diversification not only reduces risk but also opens up new opportunities for reward. Different segments of the coin market can perform differently under the same economic conditions, so a well-diversified portfolio allows you to capitalize on these variances.

In considering your investment timeline, it's important to weigh the merits of long-term versus short-term investments in coins. Long-term investments often appeal to those who see numismatics as a way to preserve wealth over time, benefiting from gradual appreciation in the value of rare and historically significant coins. This approach requires patience and a tolerance for market fluctuations, but it can be quite rewarding as rare coins tend to appreciate in value over the years. On the other hand, short-term investments can be lucrative but require a keen eye for market trends and timing. This might involve buying coins when they are undervalued and selling them when they peak in demand, a strategy that requires a good deal of market savvy and timing.

The concept of investment-grade coins is pivotal in numismatic investment. These are coins that have the potential for appreciation based on several factors, including rarity, demand, and historical importance. Identifying such coins can be the linchpin in your investment strategy. Investment grade coins are typically those that are in excellent condition, have a verified authenticity, and carry a historical significance that makes them desirable to multiple collectors. For example, a coin minted during a significant historical event or one that is part of a limited series usually holds more appeal and, consequently, more value. Ensuring that you have a solid understanding of what makes a coin desirable in the eyes of the broader collecting community can greatly enhance your ability to make sound investment decisions.

In your journey as a coin investor, staying educated and responsive to market dynamics, diversifying your holdings, understanding the investment horizon, and being able to discern the true value of investment-grade coins are all strategies that can help you navigate the complexities of the coin market. With careful planning and a robust strategy, the realm of coin collecting can be not only a fulfilling hobby but also a rewarding financial venture.

BUILDING A DIVERSE COIN PORTFOLIO

Creating a diverse coin portfolio is akin to setting a sturdy table with various dishes, each offering distinct flavors and textures. The goal is to ensure that the overall meal remains satisfying, even if one dish doesn't turn out as expected. For coin collectors, diversification involves spreading investment across different types, eras, and geographies of coins, thus balancing risk and enhancing the potential for returns. A well-rounded portfolio not only withstands market fluctuations but also provides a more engaging and rewarding collecting experience.

One effective strategy for diversification is to mix coins from different historical periods. Each era offers unique characteristics and values influenced by the socioeconomic contexts of the time. For instance, medieval coins appeal due to their historical significance and rarity, whereas modern coins are attractive due to their mint condition and technological qualities. By including coins from various periods, you mitigate the risk of your portfolio being adversely affected by period-specific market downturns. Moreover, this approach allows you to enjoy a broad spectrum of numismatic history, making your collection not only financially valuable but also intellectually stimulating.

Additionally, diversifying the types of coins in your collection can significantly enhance its resilience. This might mean combining bullion coins, which are valued primarily for their metal content, with numismatic coins, which are valued for their rarity, condition, and historical significance. Bullion coins, such as gold and silver pieces, often provide a hedge against inflation and perform well during times of economic uncertainty. On the other hand, numismatic coins can skyrocket in value due to factors like historical discoveries or shifts in collector interest. Together, these different types of coins can stabilize your portfolio against market fluctuations and ensure a more consistent overall value.

Incorporating international coins is another fruitful approach to diversification. Coins from different countries offer exposure to global numismatic practices and designs, which can be particularly advantageous during regional economic downturns. For example, if the U.S. coin market experiences a slump, your European or Asian coins might hold their value or even appreciate, balancing your portfolio's performance. Collecting international coins also opens doors to new cultural insights and historical knowledge, enriching your collecting experience and increasing the appeal and marketability of your collection to global buyers.

Monitoring and Adjusting Your Portfolio

As with any investment, regular review and adjustment of your coin portfolio are crucial to aligning it with current market trends and your personal goals. This process involves periodically assessing the performance of various segments of your collection and making informed decisions about buying, holding, or selling specific pieces. Tools and methods such as tracking auction results, staying updated through numismatic publications, and engaging with online collector communities provide valuable insights into market trends that might affect your collection.

For instance, if a particular type of coin is consistently underperforming and no longer aligns with your collecting goals, consider selling it and reinvesting in more promising areas. Conversely, if you notice an emerging trend or a gap in your collection that aligns with current market demands, acquiring coins to fill that gap could enhance both the value and the coherence of your portfolio.

It's also important to consider your personal collecting goals during these reviews. Perhaps your interests have shifted, or you've gained more knowledge in a specific area of numismatics. Adjusting your collection to reflect these changes not only ensures it remains personally rewarding but can also reinvigorate your enthusiasm for the hobby. Regularly updating your collection strategy in response to both personal and market changes ensures that your portfolio remains dynamic, relevant, and financially sound.

In conclusion, building and maintaining a diverse coin portfolio is an ongoing process that requires a strategic approach and regular adjustment. By effectively diversifying your investments and staying attuned to market trends, you can ensure that your coin collection is not only a source of personal enjoyment but also a robust investment that stands the test of time. As we transition from understanding the intricacies of building a diverse portfolio, the next chapter will explore the exciting world of coin trading and selling, where you'll learn to navigate exchanges, maximize returns, and make impactful decisions that further your numismatic journey.

CHAPTER NINE

SPECIALIZED COLLECTING

In the nuanced world of coin collecting, venturing into specialized segments can unlock a fascinating realm of unique, often overlooked treasures. Among these, error coins stand out as a captivating category. These are not your typical mint-condition pieces that shine with the flawless strokes of a well-oiled minting press. Instead, they bear the marks of mishaps—mistakes made during the minting process. Yet, it is precisely these imperfections that make them extraordinarily valuable and sought after by collectors who appreciate the beauty in the unusual. This chapter invites you to explore the intriguing world of error coins, where each misstrike tells a unique story of its creation, turning what might be seen as faults into highly prized features of your collection.

UNDERSTANDING ERROR TYPES

Error coins come into existence through a variety of mishaps in the minting process, each type offering its own story and allure. One common error is the double strike, where a coin, instead of being struck once, is hit multiple times by the coin dies, resulting in overlapping images. Then, there are off-center strikes, which occur when the coin blank is not properly aligned, and the design is consequently misprinted, sometimes dramatically so. Die varieties, another fascinating error type, emerge from anomalies in the dies themselves, such as double-dies, where a die receives an additional, misaligned impression from the engraving tool.

Each of these errors captures a moment of unintended uniqueness in the life of a coin—moments that are not meant to survive the quality control of mints. The rarity of these incidents, combined with their survival, spikes their value and appeal among collectors who are always on the lookout for something out of the ordinary.

Valuing Error Coins

The value of error coins is influenced by several factors, including the rarity and severity of the error, the coin's age, and its overall condition aside from the error. Generally, the more visually dramatic and less frequently the error is encountered, the higher the coin's value. For example, a double-struck coin where the second impression is significantly offset is typically more valuable than one with a minor misalignment. However, not all errors enhance a coin's value. Subtle errors might not be as desirable unless they are of a particular type known to be rare or sought after by specialists.

Collectors often seek out error coins that exemplify striking mistakes clearly and dramatically, as these make for more interesting displays and stories. This preference underscores the importance of visibility and recognizability in the errors that bolster a coin's collectible status and market value.

Spotting Errors

Identifying error coins requires a keen eye and knowledge of what constitutes normal and abnormal features in minted coins. Start by familiarizing yourself with the standard specifications of coins—knowing what a coin is supposed to look like is the first step in recognizing when something is amiss. Utilizing magnifying tools can help you examine coins more closely for any discrepancies.

Look for signs such as double images, off-center designs, or irregularities in the coin's rim. A digital caliper can be useful for measuring the dimensions of a coin to confirm if it has been misstruck. Remember, the authenticity of an error is crucial; some less scrupulous sellers might attempt to pass off altered or artificially damaged coins as genuine errors. Therefore, purchasing error coins from reputable dealers or verifying your finds with a professional can prevent costly mistakes.

Collecting Strategies

Building a collection of error coins involves both strategy and patience. Start by defining the focus of your collection. Do you wish to collect errors from a specific mint, or are you interested in a certain type of error? Establishing a clear focus can make your collecting efforts more organized and fulfilling. Attend coin shows and auctions where error coins are likely to appear. Networking with other error coin collectors can also provide leads on available pieces.

When assessing the worth of an error coin, consider not only its rarity but also its story—how the error might have occurred and any historical context surrounding its production. These elements can add an intangible value that makes your collection not just financially valuable but also rich in history and character.

In the realm of numismatics, error coins offer a distinctive avenue for collectors. They transform mistakes into marvels, providing collectors with not just unique items but also stories of imperfection that challenge our notions of value and perfection in coin collecting. As you delve into this specialized field, let each coin add a chapter of surprise and discovery to your numismatic journey, enriching your collection with tales of the unexpected.

EXONUMIA: TOKENS, MEDALS, AND BEYOND

When we step beyond the realm of traditional coins, we enter the diverse and fascinating world of exonumia. This term encompasses a wide range of numismatic items that are not standard currency but hold significant historical, cultural, and collectible value. Exonumia includes tokens, medals, badges, and similar objects—each with its own story and origin. These items often serve purposes beyond mere monetary transactions; they commemorate events, celebrate achievements, or function as tools in commercial exchanges where traditional currency was not practical.

Tokens, for example, have been used for everything from bus fares to arcade games. They were particularly useful in times and places where official currency was scarce or in high demand. Collecting these can provide a window into the daily lives of people in different eras and regions, reflecting local economies and social habits. Medals, on the other hand, are usually created to honor significant events or individuals. They are crafted to be keepsakes, reminders of moments that societies deem worth remembering. The designs and inscriptions on medals offer insights into the values and aesthetics of the time they were made, making them not only collectible items but also cultural artifacts.

The allure of collecting exonumia lies in its diversity and the stories these items tell. Each piece is a snapshot of a moment in history, whether it's a token from a World War II rationing system or a medal commemorating a national achievement. The variety of materials used—ranging from base metals to precious metals—and the artistry involved in their design makes exonumia a particularly rich field for collectors. The challenge and joy of exonumia collecting come from tracing these histories and understanding the contexts in which these items were made and used.

Starting an exonumia collection can be as rewarding as it is challenging, given the broad scope of items that fall under this category. Beginners might choose to focus on a specific type of item, such as military medals or transportation tokens, which can provide a manageable framework for building a collection. Local antique shops, online auctions, and specialized exonumia shows are excellent places to start looking for these items. Engaging with established collectors through clubs or online forums can also provide valuable insights and leads on where to find specific pieces. When assessing potential additions to your collection, consider not only their condition and rarity but also the story behind them—what makes them unique or historically significant. This narrative dimension can greatly enhance the personal value of your exonumia items.

Preserving and displaying exonumia presents unique challenges due to the variety of materials and sizes these items encompass. Unlike standard coins, exonumia can include large, heavy medals, delicate ribbons, or metal tokens that might be prone to oxidation. Each type of item may require different care strategies. For instance, metals may need to be kept in controlled environments to prevent tarnishing, while paper-based items like tickets or badges should be protected from light to avoid fading. Displaying exonumia effectively involves balancing visibility with preservation. Custom display cases that protect against environmental damage while allowing for clear viewing can be a worthwhile investment for serious collectors. Proper labeling and cataloging of each item can also enhance the display, providing viewers with context and enriching their appreciation of your collection.

In collecting exonumia, you are preserving fragments of history that might otherwise be overlooked. Each token, medal, or badge in your collection carries a narrative of human endeavor, cultural values, and historical moments. As you expand your collection, you delve deeper into these narratives, uncovering connections and stories that enrich your understanding of the past and its influence on the present. This exploration is not just about collecting objects; it's about discovering and preserving the diverse expressions of human life and achievement encapsulated in exonumia.

BULLION COINS: GOLD, SILVER, AND OTHER METALS

Bullion coins represent a fascinating and tangible form of investment, appealing not only to numismatists but also to those interested in precious metals as a hedge against inflation and economic uncertainty. These coins, typically made from gold, silver, platinum, or palladium, are valued primarily for their metal content. Unlike collectible coins, whose value is influenced by rarity, historical significance, or condition, the worth of bullion coins is directly tied to the current market price of the metal they contain, known as the 'spot price'. This intrinsic link to precious metals markets makes bullion coins a dynamic and potentially lucrative component of any diversified investment portfolio.

For those new to this area, understanding the basics of bullion collecting is crucial. Bullion coins are issued by governments, guaranteeing their purity and weight, which adds a layer of security for investors. Popular examples include the American Eagle series, Canadian Maple Leafs, and South African Krugerrands. These coins are typically available in various sizes, often denominated in troy ounces or fractions thereof, making them accessible to a wide range of investors. When you hold a bullion coin, you're not just holding a piece of metal; you're holding a piece of a globally recognized financial asset that can be liquidated almost anywhere in the world.

Market Factors

The values of bullion coins fluctuate with the prices of the precious metals they contain. Factors influencing these prices include global economic conditions, currency strength, interest rates, and geopolitical events. For instance, during times of economic turmoil or when inflation rates rise, precious metals like gold and silver are often seen as safe havens, leading to increased demand and higher prices. Conversely, when economies are strong and stable, the allure of these metals might diminish as other investment opportunities promise quicker or higher returns.

This volatility underscores the importance of timing in bullion investing. Keeping abreast of market trends and economic indicators can help you buy when metal prices are relatively low and potentially sell when they peak. Subscribing to financial news services, following commodities markets, and participating in financial forums can provide timely insights that inform your buying and selling decisions.

Storage and Security

Storing bullion coins safely is paramount, given their considerable value and attractiveness to thieves. Good security practices start with a quality safe that is both fireproof and waterproof. For added security, consider bolting the safe to the floor in a discreet part of your home, or even better, utilize a safe deposit box at a reputable bank or a storage facility specializing in precious metals. Insurance is another critical consideration—ensure your homeowner's policy covers the full value of your collection or obtain a separate policy for your coins.

Environmental factors also play a role in preserving your bullion coins. While less susceptible to damage than collectible coins, bullion can still suffer from improper handling and storage. Always handle coins by their edges to avoid fingerprints and scratches, and use coin capsules or cloths made from non-reactive materials to keep them pristine. These precautions help maintain the aesthetic quality of your coins, which can be important for resale value, even though it is less critical than it is for rare collectible coins.

Buying Tips

When purchasing bullion coins, understanding and assessing premiums over spot price is crucial. The premium is the amount you pay over the metal's market price, which covers the costs of production, distribution, and a small dealer markup. Comparing premiums offered by different dealers can help you find the best price, but it's also important to consider the dealer's reputation. Reputable dealers will provide transparent pricing, guaranteed coin authenticity, and secure shipping options.

Start by researching dealers who are well-established and have positive reviews from other buyers. Many dealers also offer the option to buy online, which can be convenient but requires caution—ensure the website is secure and the dealer's policies are clear. Additionally, consider attending coin shows and auctions, where you can often find competitive pricing and the added benefit of seeing the coins in person before purchasing.

In summary, collecting bullion coins is an engaging way to diversify your investment portfolio with tangible assets that hold intrinsic value. By understanding the market dynamics of precious metals, implementing secure storage solutions, and making informed buying decisions, you can enjoy the dual benefits of asset appreciation and personal satisfaction in building a collection of beautiful and valuable bullion coins. As you continue to explore this rich and rewarding field, let each acquisition be a stepping stone toward achieving both your financial and collecting goals.

COLLECTING ANCIENT COINS

The allure of ancient coins is undeniable. These coins are not merely pieces of metal but are vibrant narratives etched in alloy, telling tales of empires that shaped the world. Rome, Greece, Egypt—names that stir up images of gladiators, philosophers, and pharaohs. For collectors, these coins are a tangible connection to the distant past, an opportunity to hold history in the palm of their hand. Each coin is a relic of a bygone civilization, offering insights into the economic, political, and cultural fabric of ancient societies. The thrill of owning a

Roman denarius or an Egyptian tetradrachm goes beyond mere possession; it is about preserving a link to the ancient world and its monumental histories.

Yet, collecting ancient coins comes with its unique set of challenges, chief among them being the verification of authenticity. The market for ancient coins, while rich with opportunities, is also fraught with replicas and forgeries. The sophistication of counterfeit techniques can sometimes make it difficult to distinguish genuine artifacts from fakes. This is why authenticity verification is not just a precaution but a necessity. Engaging with reputable dealers, preferably those vetted by numismatic associations, is crucial. Many experienced dealers provide certificates of authenticity, which are invaluable. Additionally, learning about the specific characteristics of coins from different regions and eras—such as weight, diameter, and typical designs—can aid in making informed assessments about their authenticity.

The quest for ancient coins is as much about study and research as it is about collection. Delving into the history of the coins you collect enriches your understanding and appreciation of your pieces. This research might involve studying ancient numismatic literature, attending lectures and seminars, and visiting museums that house ancient collections. The more you know about the historical context in which these coins were minted and used, the more you can appreciate their value and significance. For instance, understanding the political shifts during Alexander the Great's reign can add layers of meaning to a drachma from that period, transforming it from a mere coin to a piece of historical testimony.

Conservation and care of ancient coins are paramount, given their age and historical value. These coins often come from environments that have preserved them for millennia, and inappropriate handling or storage can cause irreversible damage. It is advisable to store ancient coins in individual holders made of inert materials to avoid scratches and chemical reactions. Environmental controls are also important; extreme temperatures and humidity can accelerate deterioration. Regularly consulting with conservation experts can help maintain the integrity of these coins, ensuring that they continue to be appreciated for generations to come.

In this chapter, we have explored the fascinating world of ancient coin collecting—a pursuit that connects us to civilizations that have long vanished yet are remembered through the coins they left behind. From the bustling markets of ancient Rome to the revered temples of Egypt, each coin offers a glimpse into the lives of those who once held them. As we close this chapter, we reflect on the profound sense of continuity and history that ancient coin collecting offers. The next chapter will guide you through the modern avenues of numismatics, where innovation meets tradition, offering new perspectives and opportunities for the contemporary collector. Here, we will navigate the emerging trends and technologies that are shaping the future of coin collecting.

CHAPTER TEN

DIGITAL RESOURCES FOR COLLECTORS

In this digital age, where technology intertwines seamlessly with daily activities, integrating digital tools into your coin-collecting hobby can transform your experience from traditional to cutting-edge. Imagine having a comprehensive catalog of your collection at your fingertips, accessible at any moment and shareable with fellow enthusiasts across the globe. This isn't just convenient; it's revolutionary in managing, enhancing, and securing your valuable collection. Welcome to Chapter 10, where we explore the digital frontier of numismatics, focusing on the power and potential of online cataloging.

CATALOGING YOUR COLLECTION ONLINE

The leap from physical ledgers to digital cataloging isn't just a step toward modernization; it's a stride toward revolutionizing how you interact with your coin collection. Digital cataloging allows you to organize, search, and manage your coins with unprecedented ease and efficiency. Platforms designed for digital cataloging let you input detailed information about each coin, including images, purchase details, current values, and historical notes. This not only streamlines the organization but also enhances the interactive experience of managing your collection.

One significant advantage of digital cataloging is the ability to update and retrieve information about your coins quickly. Whether you're tracking the appreciation of your assets or recalling specific details for a potential trade, digital tools provide instantaneous access to your entire collection's data. Moreover, these platforms often include features that allow you to generate reports and analytics, giving you insights into aspects like the distribution of coin ages, origins, or even predicting trends based on your collection's historical data.

Software and Apps

Choosing the right software or app for cataloging your coin collection can significantly impact your ability to effectively manage your numismatic investments. Look for platforms that offer a user-friendly interface and robust data security measures. Features to consider include cloud-based storage, which ensures that your data is backed up and accessible from any device, and customizable fields so you can tailor the catalog to fit your specific needs.

Popular options among collectors include Numista, which provides a comprehensive toolset for cataloging and a vibrant community for trading and sharing information. Exact Change software offers detailed cataloging capabilities with extensive data about each coin type. For mobile solutions, the CoinManage app is highly regarded for its extensive database of coins from various countries and its ability to generate detailed reports.

Privacy and Security

While the benefits of digital cataloging are substantial, it's crucial to address privacy and security concerns. When selecting a cataloging platform, prioritize those that offer strong encryption and user authentication features to protect your data from unauthorized access. Be wary of services that require excessive personal information or lack clear privacy policies.

Implementing a robust password policy and enabling two-factor authentication, where available, can add an extra layer of security. Additionally, consider using a dedicated email address for your numismatic activities to safeguard your personal information further.

SHARING YOUR COLLECTION DIGITALLY

Digital tools not only facilitate the management of your collection but also open up new avenues for sharing your passion with others. Many online cataloging platforms include options for sharing your collection publicly or with specific individuals. This can be particularly enjoyable when participating in online forums or virtual clubs, where you can showcase rare finds or get insights from other collectors.

However, it's important to balance transparency and security. Consider what details you share publicly to avoid exposing too much information about valuable items. Use sharing settings to control who can see your collection and what details they can access. For an added layer of interaction, some collectors use digital platforms to create virtual tours of their collections, enhancing the communal experience of sharing their numismatic journey.

In this era, where digital convenience meets numismatic passion, leveraging online cataloging tools can significantly enhance your experience as a collector. By carefully selecting and utilizing the right digital resources, you not only safeguard and manage your collection more effectively but also share your passion with a global community of like-minded enthusiasts, all from the comfort of your home or office.

Apps and Websites Every Collector Should Know

In the expansive realm of coin collecting, staying informed and connected is paramount. Fortunately, the digital age offers an array of tools that can significantly enhance your collecting experience. Essential online resources serve as your gateway to a wealth of information, marketplaces, and forums tailored specifically for numismatists. These platforms not only streamline your pursuit of knowledge but also connect you with a global community of collectors, experts, and potential trading partners.

For anyone passionate about numismatics, familiarizing yourself with key websites is crucial. Sites like CoinWeek and NGC (Numismatic Guaranty Corporation) offer comprehensive resources that cover a wide range of topics relevant to both novice and experienced collectors. CoinWeek provides up-to-date news, articles, and guides on various aspects of coin collecting, including market trends, new coin releases, and numismatic history. Its rich content can help you stay informed about the latest developments in the world of coin collecting. On the other hand, NGC offers detailed grading services and a vast database of coin information, which is invaluable for verifying the authenticity and condition of coins. Both websites also feature high-quality images and detailed descriptions that can aid significantly in the identification and appraisal of coins.

When it comes to mobile apps, the benefits for collectors cannot be overstated. Apps like Coinoscope and PCGS CoinFacts are essential for anyone looking to streamline their collecting process. Coinoscope uses image recognition technology to identify coins from photographs. This can be particularly useful when you encounter a coin at an auction or estate sale and need to ascertain its identity quickly. The app can instantly provide you with historical data, the current market value, and even links to recent auction sales of similar coins. PCGS CoinFacts is another invaluable tool, offering a comprehensive catalog of U.S. coin issues along with high-resolution photographs and detailed historical information. This app also includes current market pricing, making it easier for you to evaluate the potential investment value of coins before adding them to your collection.

Online auction and sales platforms have transformed the way collectors buy and sell coins. Websites like eBay and Heritage Auctions provide platforms where you can participate in coin auctions from anywhere in the world. These sites offer a wide range of coins, from common pieces to rare and valuable items, making them suitable for collectors at all levels of expertise. eBay, known for its vast and diverse marketplace, allows collectors to buy and sell coins in a more informal setting. It's an excellent place for finding deals or rare pieces that might not appear in traditional auctions. Heritage Auctions, on the other hand, is one of the leading auction houses specializing in numismatic sales. It offers a more curated experience, with expertly graded coins and secure bidding processes, making it ideal for serious collectors looking to invest in high-quality numismatic items.

Navigating these digital resources effectively can significantly enhance your efficiency and success as a collector. By integrating these tools into your collecting strategy, you not only gain access to a treasure trove of information but also engage with a community that shares your passion for numismatics. Whether you are researching the history of a rare coin, assessing current market values, or looking to expand your collection through online purchases, these digital platforms offer invaluable support, helping you to advance your collecting goals and enjoy the rich world of coin collecting to its fullest.

Using Social Media to Enhance Your Collecting Experience

In today's interconnected world, social media is not just a platform for sharing life updates and catching up with friends; it's a dynamic tool that can significantly enhance your coin-collecting experience. Imagine being able to tap into a global network of coin enthusiasts and experts, gaining access to a wealth of knowledge and opportunities that were once beyond reach. Social media platforms such as Facebook, Instagram, and Twitter offer unique avenues to connect, learn, and expand your horizons in the realm of numismatics.

BUILDING A COLLECTOR NETWORK

The first step in leveraging social media for your collecting hobby is to build a network of fellow collectors and experts. This network can become your go-to resource for advice, trade opportunities, and insights into the numismatic world. Start by following well-known collectors and numismatic experts on platforms like Twitter and Instagram. Engage with their content through comments and shares, which can often lead to reciprocal interactions and the strengthening of your numismatic network.

Facebook groups and LinkedIn are particularly useful for connecting with coin-collecting communities. Look for groups with active participation and a focus on genuine sharing and discussion. Once you join, introduce yourself and your collecting interests. Participating in discussions and offering your own insights can establish you as an active and respected member of the community. Over time, these connections can lead to direct trades, joint ventures, or even invitations to exclusive numismatic events.

Discovering Rare Finds

Social media can also be an invaluable tool for discovering rare coins and exciting deals. Many collectors and dealers use platforms like Instagram to showcase their latest acquisitions or sales. By following these accounts, you can keep your finger on the pulse of what's available, often before these coins hit mainstream markets. Set up notifications for posts from key sellers and auction houses to ensure you don't miss out on potential opportunities.

Twitter's real-time updates can also be a great way to catch announcements of flash sales, auctions, or special offers from both major dealers and individual sellers. Using hashtags such as #CoinCollecting, #RareCoins, or specific coin types like #MorganDollars can help you quickly find relevant posts and listings. Remember, the key to capitalizing on these opportunities is speed and readiness; always have your resources ready for a quick assessment and purchase.

Social Media Groups

Diving deeper, specific areas of coin collecting can be explored in dedicated social media groups and forums. These groups often attract seasoned collectors and specialists who share nuanced knowledge and tips that are not available in generalist channels. For example, Facebook groups dedicated to Ancient Coins or American Silver Eagles are treasure troves of specialized knowledge, offering discussions on topics from grading nuances to historical contexts.

These groups often organize virtual meetups, webinars, or live discussions, providing platforms for deeper engagement and learning. Being an active participant in these groups not only boosts your knowledge but can also elevate your reputation within the collector community. This reputation can be crucial when seeking to buy or sell high-value coins, as trust and credibility are paramount.

Sharing Knowledge and Experiences

Finally, consider using your social media presence to share your own knowledge and experiences. Whether it's blogging about your latest coin acquisition on platforms like Medium or sharing photos of your coins on Instagram, each post contributes to the rich tapestry of the numismatic community online. Sharing not only helps others learn but also invites feedback and discussion that can enhance your own understanding and appreciation of your collection.

Creating content that adds value, such as tutorials on coin cleaning or tips on coin photography, can attract a following and establish you as a thought leader in the space. Engage regularly with your followers by responding to comments and questions. This interaction fosters a community around your content, leading to more meaningful connections and opportunities.

In leveraging social media to enhance your coin collecting experience, you're opening doors to a world of connections, knowledge, and opportunities. Each platform offers unique tools and communities that can significantly enrich your hobby, transforming it from a solitary pursuit into a shared passion with fellow enthusiasts across the globe.

ONLINE AUCTIONS AND SALES

Navigating the dynamic world of online coin auctions requires a blend of keen insight, preparedness, and strategic action. For many collectors, online auctions are a primary avenue for acquiring unique and valuable coins. The process starts long before the actual bidding begins. It involves thorough research to identify lots that not only pique your interest but also offer potential value growth. Begin by studying the auction catalog meticulously, paying close attention to the provenance, rarity, and condition reports of each coin. Utilize tools such as historical price databases to compare previous sales of similar coins. This preliminary research arms you with the knowledge needed to set a maximum bid that reflects both the coin's market value and its significance to your collection.

When placing bids, timing and tactics are crucial. Engage in the auction early by setting a preliminary bid to mark your interest, but be ready to watch the auction closely as it progresses. Some seasoned collectors recommend waiting until the closing minutes of an online auction to place your final bid. This can prevent premature price escalation and helps you avoid revealing your hand too early. However, ensure your internet connection is stable and responsive, as delays can be the difference between winning and losing a prized lot.

Selling coins online opens up your collection to a global market, significantly increasing the chances of finding interested buyers willing to pay a premium for your coins. The key to successful sales lies in how you present your coins. High-quality, clear photographs that capture the fine details and true condition of the coins are essential. Use a neutral background and natural light to enhance the visibility of important details like mint marks and any signs of wear or damage.

Listing your coins involves more than just attractive pictures. Write detailed and honest descriptions that highlight not only the coin's features but also its historical significance. Be transparent about any flaws to avoid disputes with buyers, which can harm your reputation. Pricing your coins competitively is also crucial; set prices based on current market trends, previous auction results, and the intrinsic value of the coin. Consider offering a buy-it-now option or setting a reserve price to ensure you don't sell your coins for less than their worth.

In the vast sea of online transactions, scams are, unfortunately, a reality. Protect yourself by familiarizing yourself with common fraudulent tactics such as fake listings, counterfeit coins, and phishing emails pretending to be from reputable auction sites. Always use secure payment methods and insist on well-documented shipping and return policies when buying or selling coins. Building a network of trusted fellow collectors can also provide additional layers of security, as these connections can offer second opinions and share their experiences with different sellers or buyers.

Lastly, your online reputation as a seller or buyer can significantly impact your success. Platforms typically have a feedback system where buyers and sellers rate each transaction. A positive reputation, built through consistent, honest, and professional interactions, enhances your credibility and can lead to more successful trades. Always follow through with transactions promptly, communicate clearly with other parties, and resolve any disputes amicably and professionally.

Navigating online auctions and sales effectively blends careful preparation with dynamic decision-making. By mastering these elements, you can enhance both your collection and your engagement with the global numismatic community. As you continue to explore these platforms, remember that each transaction not only adds a coin to your collection but also weaves your thread into the broader tapestry of the numismatic market.

As we conclude this chapter, we've explored how digital tools and platforms can significantly enhance your coin collecting experience. From cataloging your collection online and leveraging apps and websites to navigate auctions and sales effectively, these resources offer powerful ways to expand and manage your collection. The next chapter will delve into advanced strategies for protecting and insuring your coins, ensuring that your valuable collection is safeguarded for future generations to enjoy. This transition from digital engagement to physical preservation forms a comprehensive approach to modern numismatics.

CHAPTER ELEVEN

TURNING PASSION INTO PROFIT

Imagine the exhilaration of discovering a rare coin in your collection that has significantly appreciated in value over the years. The decision to sell such a treasure can be both thrilling and daunting. In the numismatic world, timing is more than just a tick of the clock—it's an art form that, when mastered, can dramatically enhance the profitability of your investments. This chapter delves into the nuanced dance of market timing, helping you identify the ripe moments to convert your coin collection from a passive hobby into active gains.

TIMING THE MARKET & KNOWING WHEN TO SELL

In the realm of coin collecting, the decision to sell is seldom straightforward. Timing the market for maximum profit requires a keen sense of observation and an understanding of economic cycles. Similar to the stock market, the numismatic market experiences fluctuations influenced by broader economic indicators as well as specific trends within the collecting community. A well-timed sale, when the market is buoyant, can yield substantial returns, whereas selling during a downturn might significantly undercut potential profits.

The key lies in monitoring the market continuously and being attuned to its pulse. This involves staying updated with numismatic publications, attending coin shows, and participating in collector forums. Such engagement allows you to gauge the sentiment of the market, understand what collectors are currently seeking, and anticipate shifts in demand. For instance, if there's a growing interest in coins from a particular era or a specific mint, you might find it advantageous to sell coins that align with these trends.

Recognizing Peak Value

Determining when a coin or collection has reached its peak market value is akin to catching a perfect wave for surfers—it requires skill, timing, and a bit of courage. To navigate these waters effectively, you must first understand the factors that contribute to a coin's value: rarity, demand, historical significance, and condition. A coin's peak value often coincides with heightened collector interest, perhaps due to an anniversary, rediscovery, or a surge in popularity of a certain historical period.

Implementing tools such as price tracking and historical performance charts can be invaluable. These tools allow you to visualize the price trends of your coins over time, helping you spot patterns or spikes in their value. Additionally, keeping a finger on the pulse of global economic conditions is crucial, as factors like inflation or changes in disposable income can influence collectible prices.

Economic Indicators

The broader economy plays a significant role in the timing of selling your coins. Economic indicators such as inflation rates, interest rates, and consumer spending habits can directly impact the numismatic market. For example, during periods of high inflation, tangible assets like rare coins tend to appreciate as they are seen as a hedge against the eroding value of paper money. Conversely, during economic recessions, discretionary spending on hobbies like coin collecting might decline, affecting the liquidity and prices in the numismatic market.

Keeping abreast of these indicators requires regular review of economic reports and news. Subscribing to financial newsletters, following reputable financial analysts on social media, and using economic forecasting services can provide you with insights that inform your selling strategy. This proactive approach enables you to anticipate market movements and position your coins for sale at the most opportune times.

Patience and Timing

One of the greatest virtues in coin selling is patience. The temptation to sell at the first sign of a price increase can be strong, especially if the market is volatile. However, true profits are often the reward for those who wait for just the right moment. Cultivating patience involves setting clear, strategic goals for your sale—whether it's achieving a certain return on investment, downsizing your collection, or reallocating resources toward other interests.

It's also beneficial to create a timeline for potentially selling each piece in your collection. This timeline can be adjusted based on market conditions, personal financial needs, and changes in your collecting interests. Such planning not only prepares you psychologically to part with your coins when the time is right but also ensures you are not making hasty decisions driven by short-term market fluctuations.

In navigating the complex dance of market timing, your success hinges on a blend of strategic planning, continuous learning, and an intuitive understanding of the numismatic landscape. By mastering these elements, you transform your coin collecting from a passive hobby into a dynamic and profitable venture, ensuring that each sale maximizes your financial gains while honoring the value of your cherished collection. As you move forward, remember that each decision to sell is a step toward realizing the potential of your investment, a testament to your skills as both a collector and a savvy investor.

Where to Sell

Deciding where to sell your coins is as crucial as knowing when to sell them. The choice of platform can significantly impact the ease of transaction, the price you might receive, and the speed at which you sell. Each platform, whether online marketplaces, auctions, or coin shows, comes with its unique set of advantages and challenges.

Online marketplaces offer a vast audience and the convenience of connecting with buyers directly from your home. Platforms like eBay are popular among collectors due to their broad reach and user-friendly interfaces. Here, you can create listings at your convenience, complete with photos and descriptions, and reach buyers globally. The primary advantage is the platform's massive traffic, which increases the likelihood of finding interested buyers. However, this option has its downsides. Fees can be a significant consideration as listing fees and a percentage of the sale price are often required. Additionally, the competitive nature of these platforms can drive prices down, especially if many similar items are available. Another challenge is the risk of fraud, which can be mitigated by using secure payment methods and thorough buyer vetting.

Auctions, both online and physical, provide a different selling experience. Renowned auction houses like Heritage Auctions or Stack's Bowers have a reputation for attracting serious collectors willing to pay premium prices for rare and high-quality coins. The advantage of selling through an auction is the professional handling of your coins, from cataloging to final sale, which can often result in higher realized prices due to the competitive bidding environment. However, auctions can be less predictable. There is no guarantee that your coin will sell if it does not meet the reserve price, and the timing of payment can be slower compared to direct sales. Auction houses also charge consignment fees and take a percentage of the sale price, which needs to be factored into your decision.

Coin shows provide a dynamic environment where you can interact with numerous buyers and sellers in a single venue. This option allows for immediate feedback and the ability to negotiate prices directly with buyers. The hands-on nature of coin shows makes them ideal for sellers who enjoy personal interaction and the excitement of live negotiation. On the flip side, selling at coin shows requires a more substantial time commitment and possibly travel expenses. You also compete directly with other sellers, which can require you to have standout items or competitive pricing to attract buyers.

Building a Seller's Reputation

Regardless of the platform you choose, building a solid reputation is fundamental. On online marketplaces, ensure your seller profile is complete and professional. Regularly update your listings and respond promptly and courteously to buyer inquiries. Positive reviews are gold in online selling; thus, strive to provide excellent service to receive favorable feedback. In auctions, being known as a source of high-quality and well-documented coins can make you a preferred seller. Consistency in your offerings and clarity in your consignment dealings will build your reputation over time. At coin shows, your reputation can grow through repeated fair dealings and knowledgeable interactions with other collectors. Being approachable and informed about your coins can set you apart from other sellers.

Legal Considerations

Finally, it's essential to be aware of the legal considerations involved in selling coins. Different platforms may have specific requirements or restrictions, especially when it comes to international sales. Make sure you understand the terms and conditions of the platform or venue you are using. It's also wise to familiarize yourself with any taxes or duties that might apply to your transactions. In some jurisdictions, selling collectibles like coins can have tax implications that need to be reported. Always keep thorough records of your sales, as this documentation can be crucial for tax purposes and in the event of disputes.

Navigating the various selling platforms effectively requires a blend of strategic planning, market knowledge, and adaptability. By carefully selecting your sales venue, building a strong seller profile, and adhering to legal standards, you can maximize your success in turning your numismatic passion into profit. As you continue to engage with different platforms, you'll gain insights and experiences that will hone your selling strategies, enhancing both your enjoyment and the financial rewards of your coin-collecting endeavors.

PHOTOGRAPHY TIPS FOR SELLING COINS ONLINE

Capturing the essence and true condition of a coin through photography can significantly influence the success of your online sales. High-quality images not only attract potential buyers but also provide a transparent and accurate representation of what you are offering. This transparency builds trust and can lead to higher satisfaction for the buyer, which is crucial for maintaining a strong seller reputation online. When photographing coins, several factors come into play, each contributing to the final quality of the images you produce.

Capturing Quality Images

The first step in taking high-quality photographs of your coins is ensuring that the coin is the focal point of your image. Start with a clean, lint-free cloth to gently wipe the coin, removing any dust or fingerprints that could distort its appearance in photos. It's important to handle the coin carefully by its edges to avoid any additional contact with the surface. Once the coin is prepared, set up your camera on a stable surface or a tripod to prevent any movement that could cause blurring. Using a macro lens is ideal for coin photography as it allows you to capture detailed close-ups that highlight the intricacies of the coin's design, including any mint marks, engravings, or signs of wear that are vital for assessing its condition.

Adjust the camera settings to suit the lighting and ensure you are shooting in high resolution. A higher resolution setting will capture more detail, making your images clearer and more appealing. Use the manual focus mode to control the sharpness of the image, focusing specifically on the most detailed part of the coin. If your camera has a timer function, use it. This prevents the camera from shaking when you press the shutter button, ensuring the photo remains sharp.

Lighting and Background

Lighting plays a pivotal role in coin photography. Natural light often provides the best results, offering a soft, diffused light that can illuminate the fine details of the coin without creating harsh shadows or reflections. Position your setup near a window where indirect sunlight is available, or if shooting outdoors, choose a cloudy day when the sunlight is naturally diffused. Avoid direct sunlight as it can produce glare and uneven lighting. If natural light isn't sufficient, consider using a softbox or a ring light, which provides even, steady light that can enhance the coin's features without overpowering them.

The background for your coin images should be simple and unobtrusive, ensuring that the focus remains on the coin itself. Neutral colors like black, white, or grey work well as they do not distract from the coin's details. Materials like velvet or felt can be excellent choices for a background as they not only look professional but also reduce the chance of the coin sliding. Ensure the background is clean and free from any wrinkles or debris that could detract from the overall quality of the photo.

Editing Best Practices

Once you have captured your images, editing them can enhance their clarity and attractiveness. However, it's crucial to edit responsibly to ensure the images remain a true representation of the coin's actual condition. Use photo editing software to adjust aspects such as brightness, contrast, and sharpness to bring out the details of the coin more clearly. Be cautious with filters or effects that may alter the color or texture of the coin, as these can be misleading to potential buyers.

Cropping is also an important tool in editing. Crop your images to focus closely on the coin, eliminating any distractions from the background. Ensure that all parts of the coin are visible and that the cropping does not cut off any important details. Always save your edits in a high-quality format to maintain the integrity of the image.

Photography Equipment

For those serious about coin photography, investing in good quality photography equipment can make a significant difference. A DSLR camera with a macro lens is ideal for capturing detailed close-ups necessary for coin photography. A tripod is essential for stabilizing your camera, especially in low-light conditions or when using slow shutter speeds. Additionally, consider investing in a lightbox, which provides consistent lighting and a clean, uniform background.

For those on a budget or just starting out, many modern smartphones are equipped with excellent cameras and macro capabilities suitable for basic coin photography. There are also affordable clip-on macro lenses available for smartphones that can enhance the detail captured in your photos.

By carefully managing these aspects of photography, you ensure that your coin images are not only appealing but also a true and honest representation of what you are offering, thus building trust and professionalism in your online sales endeavors.

LEGAL & ETHICAL CONSIDERATIONS IN COIN SALES

Engaging in the sale of coins, whether as an amateur enthusiast or a seasoned numismatist, involves a set of legal obligations that must be meticulously observed to ensure compliance and maintain integrity within the marketplace. One primary legal aspect revolves around the requirement for accurate disclosures. This entails providing potential buyers with comprehensive and truthful information about each coin's condition, provenance, and any other factors that may affect its value. Misrepresentation, whether by omission or fraudulent claims, can lead to serious legal consequences, including disputes, returns, and even legal actions against the seller.

Another significant legal consideration is the matter of taxes. The sale of coins, particularly when it results in a profit, may be subject to capital gains taxes depending on the jurisdiction. It is imperative to keep detailed records of each transaction, including purchase dates, prices, and sale amounts, to report any gains or losses during tax filings accurately. In some regions, there may also be specific taxes related to the sale of collectibles that need to be collected from buyers at the point of sale. Consulting with a tax professional who is familiar with local laws and regulations pertaining to collectible sales is crucial to ensure that all tax liabilities are correctly addressed and fulfilled.

Ethical Selling Practices

Maintaining honesty and transparency in representing coin conditions and history not only builds trust with buyers but also upholds the seller's reputation in the numismatic community. Ethical selling practices involve providing a detailed and accurate description of each coin's condition, including any flaws or restorations that have been made. It is also essential to verify the authenticity of the historical information provided, especially when it pertains to a coin's origin or any significant historical context that may influence its value.

Practices such as 'salting' the history of a coin—fabricating or exaggerating details to make it appear more valuable or interesting—are not only unethical but could damage the seller's credibility permanently if discovered. Sellers should strive to provide documentation or references that can verify the coin's history and authenticity. This commitment to ethical practices fosters a healthy trading environment where collectors can engage confidently, knowing that the items they are purchasing are exactly as described.

Avoiding Counterfeit Sales

The sale of counterfeit coins is a severe issue that affects both sellers and buyers and can undermine trust in the numismatic market. To prevent inadvertently selling counterfeit coins, it is crucial for sellers to implement rigorous verification processes before listing any item for sale. Utilizing services from reputable third-party grading companies can be an effective way to ensure that each coin sold is genuine and accurately graded. These companies evaluate coins not only on their condition but also authenticate them against known counterfeits.

Additionally, sellers should educate themselves about the common characteristics of counterfeit coins, which can vary significantly depending on the type and era of the coin. Regular attendance at seminars and workshops on counterfeit detection, as well as staying updated with information from numismatic associations, can enhance a seller's ability to identify and avoid fake coins. If there is ever any doubt about a coin's authenticity, it is prudent to seek expert opinions or refrain from selling the item until its authenticity can be confirmed.

NAVIGATING INTERNATIONAL SALES

Selling coins internationally introduces an additional layer of complexity due to varying regulations across countries regarding the import and export of collectibles. Sellers must be aware of and comply with customs laws in both their own country and the buyer's country. This includes accurately declaring the value and nature of the items being shipped, which can affect duties and taxes imposed on the buyer upon receipt.

Furthermore, international sales can be complicated by issues of shipping and insurance. Sellers need to ensure that coins are shipped securely and are fully insured to protect against loss or damage during transit. Utilizing reputable international shipping services that offer tracking and delivery confirmation can mitigate risks associated with international transactions.

Navigating these legal and ethical considerations is essential for any coin seller to operate successfully and responsibly in the numismatic marketplace. By adhering to these practices, sellers not only protect themselves legally and financially but also contribute to the overall trustworthiness and professionalism of the coin-collecting community. As we conclude this chapter, remember that each sale is not just a transaction but a testament to the integrity and respectability of the numismatic field. As you move forward, let these principles guide your actions, ensuring that your passion for coin collecting is matched by a commitment to ethical and responsible dealing. The next chapter will delve into safeguarding your collection, emphasizing the importance of insurance and security measures to protect your valuable investments.

CHAPTER TWELVE

SHARING YOUR PASSION

Coin collecting is more than just a personal hobby; it's a passion that can be shared across generations, creating bonds and memories that last a lifetime. As you delve deeper into the world of numismatics, you may find yourself eager to introduce this fascinating hobby to your children or grandchildren. There's a certain magic in watching young eyes light up with curiosity as they hold a piece of history in their hands—a coin that has traveled through time and space, each mark telling a story of its journey. This chapter focuses on how you can ignite and nurture the spark of coin collecting in younger family members, transforming it into a shared journey of discovery and learning.

Introducing Coin Collecting to Children and Grandchildren

The key to capturing the interest of children and grandchildren in coin collecting lies in making it an engaging and interactive experience. Consider starting with coins that feature designs that might intrigue a young mind—animals, famous historical figures, or ships. For instance, the 50 State Quarters program by the United States Mint offers a perfect starting point, with each quarter featuring distinctive designs that celebrate the history and heritage of each state. You can turn this into a fun geography lesson, locating each state on a map as you discuss the imagery on the coin.

To further enhance the experience, incorporate storytelling into your sessions. Every coin has a history, and stories about how and where a coin was used can fire a child's imagination much more than dates and facts alone. For example, Roman coins can lead to discussions about gladiators and emperors, while early American coins might spark conversations about the Revolutionary War and the founding of the United States. These stories help children form a personal connection to the coins, making the collecting experience more relatable and vivid.

Age-Appropriate Collecting Tips

When introducing coin collecting to children and grandchildren, it's crucial to tailor your approach based on their age. Younger children, for example, might enjoy a more hands-on experience, such as cleaning inexpensive coins, which provides a tactile interaction with their history. Older children and teenagers might be intrigued by the more analytical aspects of coin collecting, such as learning about grading coins or understanding market values.

Start by setting them up with a simple magnifying glass, which can be used to explore the finer details of a coin, such as mint marks and special inscriptions. This not only makes the experience educational but also turns it into a detective game where they search for small clues on each coin to learn about its origin and history.

Educational Benefits

Coin collecting is a hobby that naturally encompasses elements of history, geography, economics, and even chemistry, making it a rich educational experience. As children learn to identify where and when a coin was minted, they gain insights into historical events and economic conditions of that period. For instance, discussing why silver was used for early American coins can lead to a mini-lesson on natural resources and mining technology.

Moreover, coin collecting can help develop a child's math skills as they learn to calculate a coin's age or understand its value. It also enhances critical thinking as they assess the condition and authenticity of coins, comparing them against known standards or identifying counterfeits.

Building a Starter Collection Together

One of the most rewarding aspects of introducing coin collecting to the younger generation is the opportunity to build a starter collection together. This activity can strengthen bonds while giving them a sense of accomplishment and ownership. Begin by helping them choose a focus for their collection, whether it's coins from their birth year, coins from different countries, or thematic coins such as wildlife or leaders.

Set clear, achievable goals to keep them interested. For instance, completing a collection of current circulating coins can be a great start. Celebrate milestones along the way, perhaps by gifting them a special coin each time they achieve a goal. This not only motivates them but also shows that you value their efforts and share in their success.

By sharing your passion for coin collecting with children and grandchildren, you not only pass on valuable knowledge but also create enduring memories and instill a sense of continuity and connection to the past. This shared journey not only enhances their appreciation for history and culture but also strengthens your bond, making every coin they collect a token of cherished family moments.

CREATING A FAMILY COIN COLLECTION

Coin collecting can be a deeply personal hobby that reflects not just individual tastes but also the broader interests and heritage of a family. As you contemplate integrating this hobby more deeply into your family's activities, consider establishing a family coin collection. This collection could serve as a living archive of your family's history, interests, and shared experiences, growing and evolving with each generation. Choosing a theme for your family's collection is the first step in this process. This theme could be as broad as coins from your ancestral homeland or as specific as coins minted during significant family events like weddings or births. For instance, if your family has a strong connection to the sea, a collection themed around maritime history and featuring coins depicting famous ships, maritime explorations, or coastal cities could resonate deeply and add layers of personal significance to each piece.

Coin collecting can be a deeply personal hobby that reflects not just individual tastes but also the broader interests and heritage of a family. As you contemplate integrating this hobby more deeply into your family's activities, consider establishing a family coin collection. This collection could serve as a living archive of your family's history, interests, and shared experiences, growing and evolving with each generation.

Choosing a theme for your family's collection is the first step in this process. This theme could be as broad as coins from your ancestral homeland or as specific as coins minted during significant family events like weddings or births. For instance, if your family has a strong connection to the sea, a collection themed around maritime history and featuring coins depicting famous ships, maritime explorations, or coastal cities could resonate deeply and add layers of personal significance to each piece.

Inviting every family member to participate in this collective hobby can transform coin collecting from an individual pursuit into a family endeavor. Each member, regardless of their age, has unique perspectives and interests that can contribute to the growth and diversity of the collection. Encourage younger members to research and discover coins that align with their interests, such as technology-themed coins, if they are keen on gadgets and innovations. Older members might focus on historical or commemorative coins that connect with their life experiences or personal history. By assigning roles based on individual strengths—such as research, acquisition, or documentation—each family member can engage in a meaningful way. Regular family meetings to discuss new findings, plan acquisitions, or review the collection's status not only keep everyone involved but also reinforce the collaborative nature of the project.

Creating traditions around your family coin collection can further enhance its significance. Establishing a tradition of gifting coins on special occasions like birthdays, graduations, or anniversaries can make each addition to the collection a memorable event, celebrated and cherished by the whole family. Imagine the tradition of adding a coin to the collection every New Year's Eve, reflecting on the past year's events and how they might be represented numismatically. Such traditions help in weaving the hobby into the fabric of family life, making the collection a repository of shared memories and stories.

Documenting your family's coin collection is crucial in preserving its historical and emotional value for future generations. This documentation should go beyond mere cataloging of dates and denominations. It should capture the stories behind each coin's inclusion in the collection. Why was a particular coin chosen? What family discussions or events led to its acquisition? What does it signify about the family's interests and values at that time? Maintaining a digital or physical logbook where these narratives are recorded alongside the coins' factual data can be invaluable. This log not only serves as a guide for future additions but also as a historical document that offers insights into the family's cultural and emotional landscape over the years. Through thoughtful selection, collaborative involvement, creation of meaningful traditions, and meticulous documentation, a family coin collection can become much more than just an assortment of currency. It becomes a legacy, rich with personal and historical significance, connecting past, present, and future generations through the shared thread of numismatic passion.

PASSING DOWN YOUR COLLECTION

When you invest time, effort, and passion into building a coin collection, it often becomes more than just a hobby—it becomes a legacy. Ensuring this legacy is cherished and continues to educate and inspire future generations requires thoughtful planning and preparation. Organizing and documenting your collection meticulously is the first crucial step in preparing for its transfer. This process involves cataloging each item in your collection with detailed descriptions, including the year of minting, country of origin, historical significance, and current condition. Photographs of each coin should accompany these descriptions to provide a visual reference. Additionally, maintaining records of acquisition—such as receipts or certificates of authenticity—adds another layer of value, providing a clear trail of provenance for future custodians.

Beyond physical organization, digital documentation can significantly ease the transition of your collection to the next generation. Utilizing software designed for collectors can help digitalize your records, ensuring they are easily accessible and can be updated over time. This digital database should be backed up regularly and stored securely, with access information shared with future inheritors. This not only safeguards the information but also simplifies the management of the collection for those who inherit it, allowing them to appreciate and add to the collection without the daunting task of starting from scratch.

LEGAL AND FINANCIAL CONSIDERATIONS

Navigating the legal and financial aspects of bequeathing a coin collection is equally critical. It's advisable to have your collection appraised by a professional to determine its current market value. This appraisal is essential not only for insurance purposes while you are still the custodian but also for accurate valuation of your estate after your passing. Understanding the implications of taxes on inherited property can prevent any financial burdens on your heirs. In many jurisdictions, the value of an estate can significantly impact inheritance tax rates.

It is also prudent to consult with a legal advisor to explore the best ways to include your coin collection in your will. Specific legal instruments, like bequests or specific legacy clauses, can be used to transfer your collection according to your wishes. These legal strategies help minimize any potential disputes among heirs and ensure that your collection is handled as you intend. Additionally, discussing these plans with your heirs can alleviate any confusion and prepare them for their roles as the future custodians of your collection.

Communicating Your Wishes

Clear communication with potential heirs is paramount in legacy planning. It's essential to convey not just the logistical details about the collection and its transfer but also your emotional and educational wishes for it. Share the stories behind the coins, the lessons they embody, and your hopes for their future use. Whether you envision the collection as a continuing educational tool, a family heirloom to be passed down intact, or a means to support future financial needs, expressing these desires can help guide the next generation in their custodianship of your collection.

Creating a Trust or Foundation

For collectors who wish to extend the influence of their collection beyond their immediate family, establishing a trust or foundation can be an effective strategy. This option allows you to set more detailed parameters on how the collection should be managed and used in the future. For instance, you could stipulate that the collection be used to fund scholarships, support historical research, or be loaned to museums for public exhibition. Trusts and foundations can also offer certain tax advantages, both for you and the future beneficiaries, ensuring that more of the collection's value is preserved for its intended purpose.

Creating such a trust or foundation involves working with legal and financial professionals to ensure compliance with all applicable laws and to structure the entity in a way that best supports your goals. This path not only safeguards the collection but also elevates its purpose, turning a personal passion into a lasting philanthropic legacy.

As you reflect on the future of your collection, consider these strategies as pathways to ensure its lasting impact. By meticulously organizing, legally securing, and emotionally investing in the transition of your collection, you lay the groundwork for it to continue as a source of knowledge, joy, and inspiration. In the next chapter we will explore the intricacies of maintaining and enhancing the physical and historical integrity of your collection, ensuring its preservation for generations to come.

CHAPTER THIRTEEN

THE FUTURE OF COIN COLLECTING

As you delve deeper into the world of numismatics, it's not just the coins from the past that hold great value and intrigue; it's also the evolving trends and technologies that shape the future of coin collecting. The landscape of numismatics is continually shifting, influenced by advances in technology, changes in social interaction, and the global nature of our interconnected world. These elements not only redefine how collectors engage with their hobby but also how they preserve the legacy of historical treasures. As we look ahead, let's explore the dynamic trends that are set to revolutionize coin collecting for enthusiasts like you.

EMERGING TRENDS IN COIN COLLECTING

The infusion of technology into coin collecting is altering the traditional aspects of the hobby, making it more accessible and engaging. One of the most groundbreaking advancements is the integration of blockchain technology. Imagine a digital ledger that offers an immutable record of a coin's history, ownership, and authenticity. Blockchain can provide a new level of security and transparency in coin collecting. Each transaction or change in ownership of a coin could be recorded in a decentralized database, ensuring that the provenance and authenticity of coins are maintained transparently.

Moreover, the rise of digital currencies and tokens presents an intriguing frontier for numismatics. Collectors may soon find themselves trading or owning digital coins or tokens that represent physical coins, stored securely and traded effortlessly without the risk of physical deterioration. This digital representation could expand the hobby to those who appreciate the historical and artistic aspects of coin collecting but prefer the liquidity and practicality of digital assets.

THE ROLE OF SOCIAL MEDIA

Social media platforms are redefining community interactions, and for coin collectors, these platforms offer vibrant new avenues for engagement. Online forums and virtual clubs have become the new meeting rooms, transcending geographical barriers and creating a global community of numismatists. Through social media, collectors are not only able to share their collections and knowledge but also to foster mentorship and learning across continents.

Live streams of coin auctions, virtual tours of numismatic museums, and interactive webinars on coin grading are examples of how social media enriches the coin-collecting experience. These platforms also empower collectors to advocate for the hobby, attract new enthusiasts, and even influence trends in collecting. The interactive nature of social media could lead to a more informed and connected community of collectors, eager to share their passion and knowledge with the world.

GLOBALIZATION OF THE HOBBY

As the world becomes more interconnected, the hobby of coin collecting is experiencing unprecedented levels of globalization. Collectors are now exploring international markets more freely, discovering coins that represent diverse cultures and histories. This cross-cultural exchange enriches collections and broadens the collector's perspective on world history and art.

However, globalization also brings challenges, such as navigating international laws related to the trade and transport of collectibles. Collectors need to be more informed about customs regulations, import duties, and ethical collecting practices when acquiring coins from different countries. Despite these challenges, the increased exposure to global markets is a thrilling prospect for collectors, offering a richer tapestry of numismatic treasures to explore and cherish.

SUSTAINABILITY AND ETHICAL COLLECTING

In an era where sustainability and ethics are at the forefront of many discussions, coin collecting is also taking note. Collectors are becoming more conscious of the need for responsible collecting practices that not only preserve the coins but also the environments and communities related to them. Questions about the sourcing of coins, especially from archaeological sites, and the impact of mining metals used in coin production are prompting collectors to think more about the ethical implications of their hobby.

Provenance and legality are becoming crucial factors in the trade of numismatic items. Collectors are increasingly demanding clear documentation of a coin's history and legality, ensuring that their collections are built in a manner that respects cultural heritage and legal frameworks. This shift towards ethical collecting not only protects historical artifacts but also ensures that the hobby can be enjoyed by future generations without legal or moral complications.

As technology, social media, globalization, and ethical considerations continue to shape the landscape of coin collecting, you are at the cusp of a new era in numismatics. These trends offer exciting opportunities to deepen your engagement with the hobby, broaden your understanding of global cultures, and ensure the sustainability of your passion for future enthusiasts. As you navigate these evolving dynamics, remember that each coin in your collection does not just represent a piece of history—it's part of a continually unfolding story of human civilization, preserved through the ages by collectors like you.

CONCLUSION

As we reach the final pages of our journey together, it's essential to reflect on the expansive terrain we've traversed. From the initial steps of curating your own collection and understanding the intricacies of coin grading to the more advanced strategies of recognizing and avoiding counterfeits, and navigating the fluctuating coin market, this book has aimed to provide a thorough grounding in the world of coin collecting. We've seen how this pursuit intertwines with history, economics, and technology, providing a window into the past and a mirror reflecting our present and future.

The essence of coin collecting goes beyond the mere acquisition of rare and beautiful objects. It encompasses a deep appreciation for history and culture, an understanding of economics through the lens of numismatics, and a grasp of technological advancements that continue to shape the hobby. Each chapter of this book was designed not only to educate but also to empower you with the knowledge to make informed decisions, whether for pleasure, profit, or both.

This book serves as more than a guide; it is a gateway into the vast, interconnected world of numismatics. Through each coin, we connect with the economic currents, technological advancements, and historical events that have shaped civilizations. This journey into coin collecting thus offers a unique educational experience, enriching your understanding of the world in tangible, tactile ways.

A LIFELONG JOURNEY

I encourage you to view coin collecting not merely as a hobby but as a lifelong journey of discovery and learning. The field of numismatics is ever-evolving, with new discoveries and markets continually emerging. Each coin you encounter holds a story, waiting to be uncovered and understood. Whether you are just starting out or are an experienced collector, there is always more to learn and explore.

Now, I urge you to take whatever your next step may be in the world of coin collecting. If you haven't started yet, perhaps look into acquiring your first coin, or if you are already collecting, consider joining a coin club or delving into a specialized area of collecting. Engage with the vibrant community of collectors. Share your experiences and knowledge, and perhaps mentor someone new to the hobby. Your participation enriches not only your own life but also the broader community of collectors.

I also encourage you to share your passion for coin collecting with younger generations. Introduce them to the joys and lessons that can be found in every coin. Teach them about history, economics, and art through these small but significant tokens of our past. In doing so, you help ensure that the valuable lessons and joys of coin collecting continue to inspire and educate far into the future.

CONCLUSION

Thank you sincerely for joining me on this journey through the pages of this book. Your enthusiasm and curiosity are what keep the spirit of coin collecting alive and vibrant. I am profoundly grateful for your time and interest, and I hope that you have found this book to be both informative and inspiring. May your path through the world of coin collecting bring you much joy, knowledge, and connection.

Happy collecting!

Now that you have everything you need to start your coin-collecting journey, it's time to pass on your newfound knowledge and show other readers where they can find the same help.

Simply by leaving your honest opinion of this book on Amazon, you'll show other budding coin collectors where they can find the information they're looking for and pass their passion for coin collecting forward.

Thank you for your help. The joy of coin collecting is kept alive when we pass on our knowledge – and you're helping me to do just that.

or click here on your devices

- Happy Collecting

REFERENCES

The Royal Mint. (n.d.). The beginners guide to coin collecting. Retrieved from https://www.royalmint.com/discover/coin-collecting/beginners-guide-to-coin-collecting/

Provident Metals. (n.d.). Bullion vs. numismatic coins. Retrieved from https://www.providentmetals.com/knowledge-center/precious-metals-resources/bullion-vs-numismatic-coins.html

Invaluable. (n.d.). How to grade coins: Tips for beginner professional coin graders. Retrieved from https://www.invaluable.com/blog/the-collectors-guide-to-coin-grading/

U.S. Mint. (n.d.). Caring for your coin collection. Retrieved from https://www.usmint.gov/learn/collecting-basics/caring-for-your-coin-collection

PCGS. (n.d.). PCGS coin price guide: The industry standard for US coins. Retrieved from https://www.pcgs.com/prices/us

U.S. Mint. (n.d.). Mint marks. Retrieved from https://www.usmint.gov/learn/collecting-basics/mint-marks#:~:text=Mint%20marks%20are%20letters%20that,each%20of%20the%20Mint%20facilities.

The Collector. (n.d.). 10 most important ancient coins ever minted. Retrieved from https://www.thecollector.com/important-ancient-coins/

Eyes of Unity. (n.d.). Minting innovation: How technology is transforming coin production. Retrieved from https://medium.com/@eyesofunity/minting-innovation-how-technology-is-transforming-coin-production-9832ad8b2d2f

U.S. Money Reserve. (n.d.). Sheldon coin grading scale. Retrieved from https://www.usmoneyreserve.com/news/executive-insights/sheldon-coin-grading-scale/

Oxford Gold Group. (n.d.). How to find the best coin grading services in the market. Retrieved from https://www.oxfordgoldgroup.com/articles/best-coin-grading-service/

The Spruce Crafts. (n.d.). Coin grading made simple. Retrieved from https://www.thesprucecrafts.com/coin-grading-made-simple-768384

Numismatic News. (n.d.). Coin grading skills prevent costly mistakes. Retrieved from https://www.numismaticnews.net/archive/coin-grading-skills-prevent-costly-mistakes

NGC. (n.d.). Counterfeit detection. Retrieved from https://www.ngccoin.com/resources/counterfeit-detection/

Microscope World. (n.d.). Microscopes for coin collectors. Retrieved from https://www.microscopeworld.com/t-coin_collecting.aspx

ScienceDirect. (n.d.). Counterfeit coin of the realm – Review and case study. Retrieved from https://www.sciencedirect.com/science/article/pii/S1350630706002044

The Spruce Crafts. (n.d.). Top 4 coin grading and authentication services. Retrieved from https://www.thesprucecrafts.com/coin-grading-services-768302

Wikipedia. (n.d.). History of coins. Retrieved from https://en.wikipedia.org/wiki/History_of_coins

Bankrate. (n.d.). 9 of the world's most valuable coins. Retrieved from https://www.bankrate.com/investing/worlds-most-valuable-coins/

SpringerLink. (n.d.). The role of money in the economies of ancient Greece and Rome. Retrieved from https://link.springer.com/10.1007/978-981-13-0596-2_46

Cambridge Core. (n.d.). Rethinking numismatics: The archaeology of coins. Retrieved from https://www.cambridge.org/core/journals/archaeological-dialogues/article/rethinking-numismatics-the-archaeology-of-coins/1F52234518C8BEFCC0BF6064B3BB9FFF

U.S. Mint. (n.d.). Caring for your coin collection. Retrieved from https://www.usmint.gov/learn/collecting-basics/caring-for-your-coin-collection

REFERENCES

APMEX. (n.d.). How to insure a coin collection. Retrieved from https://learn. apmex.com/learning-guide/coin-collecting/how-to-insure-a-coin-collection/

NGC. (n.d.). NCS conservation: Environmental damage. Retrieved from https://www.ngccoin.com/news/article/5630/ncs-conservation/

Federal Trade Commission. (n.d.). Hobby Protection Act. Retrieved from https://www.ftc.gov/legal-library/browse/rules/hobby-protection-act

Bottom Line Inc. (n.d.). Why you should join a coin-collecting club (and the best ones). Retrieved from https://www.bottomlineinc.com/blogs/money-connoisseur/best-coin-collecting-clubs

American Numismatic Association. (n.d.). Attending your first coin show. Retrieved from https://blog.money.org/coin-collecting/first-coin-show

Quora. (n.d.). How do people keep their coin collections safe from theft? Retrieved from https://www.quora.com/How-do-people-keep-their-coin-collections-safe-from-theft

Numismatic News. (n.d.). Market update. Retrieved from https://www. numismaticnews.net/coin-market/update

Coin Collecting. (n.d.). 4 steps to determine what your coin is worth. Retrieved from https://www.coincollecting.com/4-steps-to-determine-what-your-coin-is-worth

American Numismatic Association. (n.d.). The Numismatist magazine: Coin collecting & numismatics. Retrieved from https://www.money.org/numismatist/

Personal Finance Blogs. (n.d.). Building a diverse and profitable coin portfolio. Retrieved from https://personalfinanceblogs.com/coin-collecting-101-building-a-diverse-and-profitable-coin-portfolio/

The Spruce Crafts. (n.d.). How to find rare error coins in circulation. Retrieved from https://www.thesprucecrafts.com/find-rare-error-coins-in-circulation-768762

Rare Coin Store. (n.d.). Exonumia: An introduction to the world of numismatics. Retrieved from https://rarecoin.store/en/blog/what-are-exonumia-and-how-does-collecting-exonumia-differ-from-numismatic-items/#:~:text=Exonumia%20refers%20to%20the%20study,that%20are%20not%20legal%20tender.

American Numismatic Association. (n.d.). Tips for buying and selling bullion. Retrieved from https://www.money.org/selling-and-trading-tips/

Forum Ancient Coins. (n.d.). Ancient coin authentication 101. Retrieved from https://www.forumancientcoins.com/NumisWiki/view.asp?key=Ancient%20Coin%20Authentication%20101

OpenNumismat. (n.d.). OpenNumismat - Free coin collecting software. Retrieved from http://opennumismat.github.io/

The Spruce Crafts. (n.d.). Top 10 websites for coin collectors & enthusiasts. Retrieved from https://www.thesprucecrafts.com/best-coins-sites-on-the-web-3898464

PCGS. (n.d.). How to avoid purchasing counterfeit coins. Retrieved from https://www.pcgs.com/news/how-to-avoid-purchasing-counterfeit-coins

Marketplace. (2022, May 2). Coin collecting is big business on social media. Retrieved from https://www.marketplace.org/2022/05/02/coin-collecting-is-big-business-on-social-media/

Douglas Winter Numismatics. (n.d.). Timing in the coin market. Retrieved from https://raregoldcoins.com/blog/market-blog/timing-in-the-coin-market

Yahoo Finance. (n.d.). 5 best places to sell rare coins and paper money. Retrieved from https://finance.yahoo.com/news/5-best-places-sell-rare-120015687.html

Artemis Collection. (n.d.). A brief guide to coin photography. Retrieved from https://artemis-collection.com/photography/a-brief-guide-to-coin-photography/

GovInfo. (n.d.). Investing in collectible coins. Retrieved from https://www.govinfo.gov/content/pkg/GOVPUB-FT-PURL-gpo17841/pdf/GOVPUB-FT-PURL-gpo17841.pdf

U.S. Mint. (n.d.). Coin activities for kids. Retrieved from https://www.usmint.gov/learn/kids/resources/coin-activities

American Numismatic Association. (n.d.). Coins in the classroom. Retrieved from https://www.money.org/numismatic-events-coins-in-the-classroom/

BullionMax. (n.d.). What to do if you inherited a coin collection. Retrieved from https://www.bullionmax.com/kb/inherited-coin-collection/

Satta Blog Post King. (n.d.). The impact of blockchain technology on authenticating rare coins. Retrieved from https://sattablogpostking.com.in/?p=738

Marketplace. (2022, May 2). Coin collecting is big business on social media. Retrieved from https://www.marketplace.org/2022/05/02/coin-collecting-is-big-business-on-social-media/

Maximize Market Research. (n.d.). Coin collection market: Analysis and forecast 2024-2030. Retrieved from https://www.maximizemarketresearch.com/market-report/coin-collection-market/194419/

MDPI. (n.d.). Sustainable approach to metal coin canceling methods. Retrieved from https://www.mdpi.com/2071-1050/16/6/2322

Xx89 Washington Quarter Dollar 1965 - Present.jpg. (n.d.). In Wikimedia Commons. Retrieved July 7, 2024, from https://commons.wikimedia.org/wiki/File:Xx89_Washington_Quarter_Dollar_1965_-_Present.jpg

1955 doubled die Lincoln cent.jpg. (n.d.). In Wikimedia Commons. Retrieved July 7, 2024, from https://commons.wikimedia.org/wiki/File:1955_doubled_die_Lincoln_cent.jpg

1959 sovereign Elizabeth II obverse.jpg. (n.d.). In Wikimedia Commons. Retrieved July 7, 2024, from https://commons.wikimedia.org/wiki/File:1959_sovereign_Elizabeth_II_obverse.jpg

Japan, 1889 - 1 yen, Emperor Meiji.jpg. (n.d.). In Wikimedia Commons. Retrieved July 7, 2024, from https://commons.wikimedia.org/wiki/File:Japan,_1889_-_1_yen,_Emperor_Meiji.jpg

1901 UN PESO libertad republic mexicana.jpg. (n.d.). In Wikimedia Commons. Retrieved July 7, 2024, from https://commons.wikimedia.org/wiki/File:1901_UN_PESO_libertad_republic_mexicana.jpg

Chinese Money 18 - Song-Yuan Amulet Coin.jpg. (n.d.). In Wikimedia Commons. Retrieved July 7, 2024, from https://commons.wikimedia.org/wiki/File:Chinese_Money_18_-_Song-Yuan_Amulet_Coin.jpg

NNC-US-1913-5C-Buffalo Nickel (TyII-line).jpg. (n.d.). In Wikimedia Commons. Retrieved July 7, 2024, from https://commons.wikimedia.org/wiki/File:NNC-US-1913-5C-Buffalo_Nickel_(TyII-line).jpg

NNC-US-1907-G$20-Saint Gaudens (Arabic).jpg. (n.d.). In Wikimedia Commons. Retrieved July 7, 2024, from https://commons.wikimedia.org/wiki/File:NNC-US-1907-G$20-Saint_Gaudens_(Arabic).jpg

Y2klibholoobv.jpg. (n.d.). In Wikimedia Commons. Retrieved July 7, 2024, from https://commons.wikimedia.org/wiki/File:Y2klibholoobv.jpg

International Precious Metals. (n.d.). *Are graded coins worth more?* International Precious Metals. https://www.preciousmetals.com/blog/post/getting-coins-graded.html